HAUNTED
CHARLOTTESVILLE
and Surrounding Counties

HAUNTED
CHARLOTTESVILLE
and Surrounding Counties

Susan Schwartz

PHOTOGRAPHS BY CLIFF MIDDLEBROOK JR.

SCHIFFER
PUBLISHING

4880 Lower Valley Road · Atglen, PA 19310

Cover design by Molly Shields
Type set in Minion Pro, Haunt AOE & Avance

ISBN: 978-0-7643-5759-6
Printed in the United States of America

Published by Schiffer Publishing, Ltd.
4880 Lower Valley Road
Atglen, PA 19310
Phone: (610) 593-1777; Fax: (610) 593-2002
E-mail: Info@schifferbooks.com
Web: www.schifferbooks.com

For our complete selection of fine books on this and related subjects, please visit our website at www.schifferbooks.com. You may also write for a free catalog.

Schiffer Publishing's titles are available at special discounts for bulk purchases for sales promotions or premiums. Special editions, including personalized covers, corporate imprints, and excerpts, can be created in large quantities for special needs. For more information, contact the publisher.

We are always looking for people to write books on new and related subjects. If you have an idea for a book, please contact us at proposals@schifferbooks.com.

DEDICATION

This book is dedicated to my husband, Michael, and my son, Timothy, who always push me to be better than I was yesterday. They fill me with hope, love, and a sense of wonder about the world around me. I love you both very much.

Michael, let's keep those black-eyed peas in the freezer a little longer.

Timothy, keep breaking a leg out there.
I am so very proud of you.

In Memoriam

Cliff Middlebrook Sr.

1934–2014

In loving memory of our father, Cliff Middlebrook Sr., who loved to go ghost hunting with me at various sites. Fascinated when we would find a ghost in our pictures, he surely would have had a wonderful time visiting all the historical sites mentioned in the book. Daddy never met a stranger, and he would always delight people with tales from his days of traveling and growing up in the country. I hope he is now causing as much mischief and merriment in Heaven as he did here on Earth.

CONTENTS

FOREWORD

Is Virginia truly haunted? Yes, it is.

Williamsburg brags about being the most haunted area in the commonwealth of Virginia, holding several ghost tours all year-round. Tourists stay in hotels where they can witness spectral colonists or Civil War soldiers walk through walls. Stories of Bigfoot, Wampus Cat, spectral black dogs, phantom soldiers, and witches stalking the mountains of western Virginia, southwestern and southeastern sections, and even down at the Tidewater region have been told since the first colonists settled the land. Then there's Petersburg and the Tri-Cities area, which I believe to be the most haunted section of Virginia, maybe due to the Siege and the battles that happened there. But these are not the only ghost-ridden territories.

Susan Schwartz has tackled the monumental job of discovering what haunts Charlottesville (colloquially called C'ville), and the towns, villages, and countryside in its surrounding area. Charlottesville is famous for the Festival of the Book, which happens each March, drawing scores of authors and readers to the event. Susan's book is about the mysteries of local specters, monsters, and urban legends, plus the sense of history that molded this area into what we know today. Susan brings all the undead to life in the stories she has ferreted out, even daring to do a couple of investigations at night, such as at the Exchange Hotel Museum in Gordonsville. Charlottesville has the University of Virginia, founded in 1819 by Thomas Jefferson, where those who might have taken classes in the past may still be there, but in vaporous form. This may even include Edgar Allan Poe! There's Jefferson's own Monticello, where his romance with slave Sally Hemings began, but other phantoms may still roam the house or property for one reason or another. Susan says that Michie Tavern has great food and that it also has ghosts too. There isn't an acreage in this town or all the surrounding lands that doesn't have a haunt or two.

Virginians, the next time you want to do the touristy thing and take a day trip, get Susan's book and use it to visit the area a little differently. For those of you not from outside the commonwealth, Susan's book will steer your straight into what ghostly activities you might want to partake of while visiting specific locations.

See history through the dead's eyes, eat where ghosts might dine, and maybe, just maybe, touring Monticello, the Exchange Hotel, Bear Creek Lake State Park (where staying in their cabins offer more than rustic peace, but spirits too), and the other places, don't be surprised if you see something wispy out of the corner of your eye. It's not dust, pollen, or even something substantial there; it's only history haunting you. So turn that page and begin Susan Schwartz's ghostly tour of a region still populated by the dead.

Pamela K. Kinney

Author of the ghost books *Paranormal Petersburg, Virginia, and the Tri-Cities*, *Haunted Richmond*, *Haunted Richmond II*, and *Haunted Virginia: Legends, Myths and True Tales*, and the fiction books *How the Vortex Changed My Life* and *Spectre Nightmares and Visitations*

ACKNOWLEDGMENTS

Many people who helped me get this book off the ground need to be recognized. I want them to know how truly grateful I am for their assistance in making a dream of mine come true.

I first want to give a huge thank you to Pete Schiffer and Dinah Roseberry for taking a chance and giving me this wonderful opportunity to fulfill a goal of mine. Dinah is one of the nicest people I have met; she is always helpful and full of great suggestions.

I need to give a long overdue thanks to Pamela K. Kinney. Without her prodding, I may never have gotten this book going. I would say it is all her fault, but she has been a wonderful mentor while I have been working on this book. She also helped edit some of the chapters.

I also need to thank my talented brother, Cliff Middlebrook. He has traipsed many cemeteries and other haunted places with me throughout the writing of this book. He has only added to the wonder of the pages that follow with his awesome photographs of the locations we visited on many weekends.

I owe much gratitude to my husband, Michael. He helped me edit and throw ideas around while writing, and he drove me all over creation some days so I could meet with certain establishments.

My son, Timothy, improved my author website immensely. He also helped me edit the finished book. I am so thankful for his assistance and expertise.

I want to express gratitude to my sister, Carolyn Becker, who drove me all over Louisa and Mineral to get pictures and do research. She also made an awesome poster for me to display at book signings.

I owe much thanks to Maggie King and Carol Smith for writing me some great recommendations for the back cover. Carol also edited some chapters to help with wording.

I need to thank my writer's group from the Virginia Writers Club. Without these wonderful mentors, I would have never learned how to write with the style and grace that I do. They are still an inspiration to me today. We lost Bill Denton in August 2015; however, he remains a shining beacon to me. I just hope I can live up to his expectations. He was my adopted big brother and the kindest man you would ever want to meet. I hope he is marking up the Big Book with his red pen these days. He and a few other great writers (Charlie Finley, Patsy Anne Bickerstaff, Preston Nuttall, Jim Cotter, and Sara Rupnik) taught me to write, providing me with constant encouragement and constructive criticism.

I also wish to thank those places that opened their doors so I could interview them and take pictures of the properties. There were some that did not want to participate, but most were welcoming and very hospitable. The list includes Rita Sausmikat and Addison Thompson at Tuckahoe Plantation; Cindy Conte and Miss May at Michie Tavern; Todd and Kendra Tribble at Tribble Farm; President Casteen,

Nancy Ingram, and Melissa Loggans at the University of Virginia; Amanda Kutch for her wonderful and informative tours of Maplewood, Oakwood, and Riverview Cemeteries; Paul Jones at the Old Albemarle County Jail; Lee Wilcox and Zachary Pittard for their valuable contributions on the Saylor's Creek Battlefield; Jim Godburn for his informative tour of Hillsman House; Liz and Joe Konan at Troy's Market & Deli; Trisha Johnson at the Old Fluvanna Jail and Courthouse; Matt, Kim, and Phillip at Willow Grove Inn; Jack and Pat North at Mayhurst Inn; Brittany and Allison at Ash Lawn–Highland; Margaret O'Bryant at the Albemarle Historical Society; Angel May and Missy Sykes at the Exchange Hotel; Candace DeLoach and Steve Allen at the Inn at Court Square; Amanda Hester at Comyn Hall; Sandy Dulaney at Swannanoa Palace; Jen and Leslie Tal at Mark Addy Inn; Denise Smith and Tony at Graffiti House; Andrew Ferlazzo and Kevin Scott at Grass Rootes Restaurant; Martha Breeden and Carol Milkes at the Madison County Historical Society; Lena Scherquist at Salubria Manor; Deon and Max Abrams at Grayhaven Winery; and Paige and Steven Castello and John Maddox for Mark Addy Inn.

Lastly, I need to thank you, the reader, for taking a chance on me and reading about the fascinating places presented here. I truly appreciate your support. I had so much fun exploring these locations, some historic and some private homes; all were filled with history and a charm that invites you back again and again. I hope you will visit some of these places and open your eyes to the wonder that is out there beyond the veil.

INTRODUCTION

Being a lifelong taphophile, I have always enjoyed traipsing through graveyards and cemeteries, taking pictures of the ornate stones and obelisks in hopes of catching a glimpse of the other side. I also like the quiet and peaceful nature of the setting.

My first ghost hunt was at Cold Harbor Cemetery in Mechanicsville, Virginia, with Pamela K. Kinney. My father and I rode over to see the cemetery, since it is known to be very haunted. Many visitors take pictures showing soldiers still fighting the battle, and notice the smell of fired cannons. There is also a feeling of someone watching you the whole time you are visiting.

We met up with Pamela and headed off into the cemetery. I sometimes get pushes and pulls or chills when something supernatural is nearby. I felt all of these many times that day. Perhaps the weirdest experience I had happened when I walked over to a gravesite completely covered by brush and debris. I cleaned it off so you could see the man's name on the stone. At that precise moment, I froze. I was aware that Pamela and my father were talking, but I couldn't say anything. An ice-cold feeling ran through me over the course of a few seconds. When I told Pamela about it, she said a ghost might have walked through me.

Have you ever seen or heard a ghost? I have taken many pictures of questionable specters, and I have heard them call me. Please believe me, I am a huge skeptic and still look for corroborating evidence. My brother and I have carefully chosen all the pictures in this book by enlarging them and making sure that they were true to the nature of the genre. We had plenty of iffy pictures, but we chose the ones that really showed what we thought were spiritual images. Will these change your mind about the afterlife? Maybe, maybe not. Each of us must determine what we believe and how far we are ready to take that conviction. I know there is something beyond death; many people do not. It is fear of our own mortality that makes you take such a strong stand against it.

What exactly is a ghost? Many people say they are spirits who weren't ready to cross over and had unfinished business, or they are reliving a past event over and over. They can appear as shadows, orbs of light, mist, wavy lines through pictures, and even specific scents. You can catch them in a reflection of a mirror. Those images make us question our belief system and what really goes on behind the veil of death.

The areas chosen for this work have come from a vast section of the commonwealth I have traveled and explored most of my life. Charlottesville and the surrounding counties cover a vast amount of land, houses, and cemeteries. All these areas are rich with legends and stories that have been passed down from generation to generation. I have tried to weave them both into fascinating history and the current haunting situation. I placed them in a specific order to assist in your exploration of the different counties.

The most fascinating concept is how many legends and stories Virginia has inside its borders, from the Civil War to the presidents who lived in the Old Dominion. It really is interesting to note how many of these historic homes, cemeteries, businesses, and people are interconnected somehow. As we all know, there is no such thing as coincidence. Think about that while you are reading about the locations in the book.

It is also my hope you will visit some of the sites mentioned in this book, and develop your own opinion about that ghost that is lurking over your shoulder right now.

IMPORTANT NOTICE: PLEASE DO NOT TRESPASS ON ANYONE'S PROPERTY UNLESS GIVEN SPECIFIC PERMISSION BY THE OWNERS.

1.
ALBEMARLE

Castle Hill entrance

CASTLE HILL MANOR

Castle Hill was home to Dr. Thomas Walker and his wife, Mildred Thornton Meriwether, during the late 1700s. The good doctor built it in 1764 in colonial tradition. It is now a privately owned 600-acre plantation sitting at the bottom of the Southwest Mountains about 3.6 miles from Monticello. The history of the manor is as fascinating as the people who have stayed there over the years.

Banastre Tarleton, a British colonel, and his men were stuck at the manor in June 1781. Dr. Walker was the cause of this unexpected stay. If he had not intervened, the history of the United States may have changed forever. Dr. Walker held up the British troops so Jack Jouett could ride forward, Paul Revere style, and warn key people of Tarleton's approach. These included Thomas Jefferson, Benjamin Harrison, Patrick Henry, and Richard Henry Lee. Jouett had been staying at the Cuckoo Tavern in Louisa when he heard talk of Tarleton wanting to capture Charlottesville and the important political leaders who governed Virginia. Jouett rode forty miles to Castle Hill and warn Dr. Walker.

Once Dr. Walker and his wife knew of the impending capture, they waited for Tarleton and his men to arrive at their home. At daybreak, they reached Castle Hill and demanded sustenance. They gave the men spiked drinks and delayed feeding them as long as possible. Tarleton even complained about the slow service he was getting from the kitchen staff. They finally fed the whole army; however, by the time they were finished eating, Jouett had arrived at Monticello to warn Jefferson of the coming storm.

In 1824, William Cabell Rives built an addition onto the home after part of it had been burned down by Native Americans. Castle Hill descended through the family down to his granddaughter, Amelie, who was an author in her own right. Her most famous novel, *The Quick and the Dead*, was published in the late 1880s, and she was an instant success at twenty-five.

After she divorced her first husband, she married Prince Pierre Troubetzkoy, a painter in Russia. They entertained many distinguished guests over the years they lived at Castle Hill, including authors, statesmen, generals, and presidents. It was a warm and exuberant place to stay while traveling to Charlottesville or farther. It was also in the early 1900s that some of the manifestations started to take place in the manor.

The Troubetzkoys received many reports of guests hearing footsteps traveling up and down the stairs each night. Some complained of furniture being rearranged throughout the night. Some could hear people talking outside their room, and when they went to tell the people to stop, there was no one in the hallway. Many guests noted the smell of roses on the staircase, but they could never find anyone who was wearing perfume or cologne with the same odor (Shadowlands Haunted Places Index 1998).

A former maid came forward in 1982 and admitted that something grabbed her leg many times while walking through the house or sleeping in her bed. She also heard complaints of a loud, raucous party downstairs, complete with doors opening, glasses clinking, and people laughing. When the area was investigated, there was not a soul present.

There was one spirit who stayed sequestered in the Pink Bedroom. On the basis of descriptions of the apparition, Mrs. Troubetzkoy thought it could be her aunt, Amelie Louis Sigourney. The poor woman drowned when their ship to France sank in 1870. She could be very jovial to some guests and downright mean to others. She was dressed in period clothing and held a tiny fan. Several guests met up with her while in the room, and they all left in a hurry, swearing never to return. Many said that she told them to go away and that they couldn't stay there any longer. On an opposite note, some guests have slept in the room with no issue at all. The spirit must be finicky as to who can stay there and who cannot (Holzer 1998).

CASTLE HILL
PRIVATE RESIDENCE

CASTALIA MANOR

Front gate to Castalia Manor

Built in 1850, Castalia Manor is a three-story home near the center of Charlottesville. Its red-brick chimneys will catch the viewer's eye, as will the large wraparound porches (Taylor 1992). Being a historic home, there are many spooky happenings within the manor. These include people in period clothing appearing and disappearing, unexplained footsteps throughout the home, dishes being thrown all over, clothes strewn through the house, and doors opening by themselves (Derby 2013).

The most common occurrence is the horseback rider who acts like an escort for people coming to see the manor. Many have seen the spectral rider, who then vanishes, and no one can find him.

There is also a sad female who inhabits the house. Starting as far back as the 1920s, people have described feeling or seeing this lady. She is described as having a small frame with brunette hair that is pulled back into a bun. She also wears a shawl and a striped sort of dress. The residents of the home said it appeared as if she was organizing papers when they saw her. Simultaneously, they would begin to hear the sounds of onions being chopped. She walked over to where a resident was sitting and vanished (Taylor 1992).

Another relative heard the unexplained footsteps around 5:00 a.m. She thought it was her husband pacing around the floor. She went to investigate and discovered her husband still in his bed asleep. Following that night, she continued to hear the footsteps at the same time every morning. The owners told her not to worry; it was just their friendly ghost visiting her (Taylor 1992).

Another relative told a story about two girls in the Chintz Room on a cold winter's night. Sometime after midnight, one of the girls awoke after hearing a noise.

She thought her friends had gotten up to get a drink. Her friend apparently had the same thought. When they switched on the light, they discovered the clothes they had hung over a chair were now thrown on the floor, and the chair by the fireplace also had an open book sitting on it that wasn't there before they went to bed. They both complained the room was freezing at the time, even though they had a warm fire going.

One of the girls also wound up calling her parents to come home from a party because she had heard a loud crash on the second floor. She brought her dog, Flossie, with her to investigate the noise. The dog started up the stairs to attack the intruder; however, she turned around and came flying back down the stairs looking scared and whimpering. The girl stayed downstairs until her parents returned. Upon searching the upstairs, her parents found nothing out of order that could have scared the dog (Taylor 1992).

The Chintz and Lavender Rooms were also locations for assorted occurrences. An older woman with a cap was seen in these rooms as unexplained noises and loud crashes were heard. When the owners investigated to see what had been damaged, there was nothing out of place. Lights would turn on in specific rooms even when no one had been near the switches. The Lavender Room was a favorite spot for the spirit of the older woman. One day, they decided to check out the room to make sure nothing was amiss, since it had not been opened for some time. They found a scarf and the bedspread in a heap on the floor.

Noted investigator Hans Holzer came to visit the manor and brought a psychic with him to find an explanation for the strange occurrences. Apparently, the older woman was waiting for her husband to return from a battle. (Holzer wondered if the rider on the horse that led people to the house might have been the man returning.) The more agitated and worried she became, the more she would pace across the floor, which explains the footsteps. The old woman finally passed away, but she never left the house. She refused to acknowledge that both she and her husband had died. The psychic gently explained the situation and that she could now see her husband again if she crossed over to the light. After this transpired, she was not seen again (Holzer 1999).

It is a happy note for this story to end here. The woman finally found peace and her love. These types of cases always remind us that there is more across the veil than we really know.

CASTALIA MANOR
Private residence

MONTICELLO

Beginning construction in 1770, Monticello became home to Thomas Jefferson, the third president of the United States. Monticello was built in two phases. The first phase consisted of brickwork and construction of the home. This included eight rooms surrounded on the outside by Doric, Ionic, and neoclassical architecture. This first part also included a large parlor on the ground floor that had a dining room and another room surrounding it. The second floor contained a spacious study and two bedrooms.

As construction moved forward, phase two started. In the year 1790, a major renovation began. Excavation of cellars to make more room underneath the house commenced. The dome on top was built in 1800, with eight skylights added to the ceiling for the ambiance of natural light. Jefferson came up with the idea after reading through Philibert Delorme's book on French architecture.

The house was completed in 1809, some thirty-nine years after it was started. Jefferson retired to Monticello after being in Washington for the prior eight years. He died on July 4, 1826—a historically coincidental date. It was both the fiftieth anniversary of the signing of the Declaration of Independence and the day his good friend John Adams, second president of the United States, also died.

There are many ghost stories that surround the magnificent home settled in the mountains of Charlottesville. There is a sitting room on the first floor that his oldest daughter, Martha Jefferson Randolph, employed as a classroom to teach reading and writing to her children, as well as manage the servants that worked at Monticello (Miller and Miller 2016).

In 2015, a security guard walking through Monticello after closing time stopped in the sitting room to take a picture of the gorgeous sunset out one of the windows. All of a sudden, the camera froze and shut completely off. He then heard a loud whispered "NO!" behind him. No one else was in the room.

Some visitors have taken a picture of a ten-year-old boy who peers out of the second-floor window. He is wearing a uniform and a tricornered hat. His identity is unknown.

Jefferson was known to whistle or hum a tune while he went about his working day. He could be heard in the house and all over the grounds, especially in the gardens. After Monticello closes for the day, there have been reports of phantom footsteps as well as whistling near the gardens and in the house. Some have even seen Jefferson's ghost at times performing the tune (Haunted Places 2016d).

There is one more story about Jefferson that must be added here, although it doesn't have to do with Monticello. It concerns an interesting event in the city of Fredericksburg. A lawyer spotted the apparitions of Thomas Jefferson and James Monroe at the front door of his law office. He stated that they were dressed in colonial attire and having an argument outside his office. He went down to approach the men, and they simply vanished by walking right *through* the wooden door into the law office. He ran to ask some coworkers where they had gone once inside, but no one else had seen them (Taylor 1992).

MONTICELLO
931 THOMAS JEFFERSON PARKWAY
CHARLOTTESVILLE, VA 22902
434-984-9800
WWW.MONTICELLO.ORG
MANY TOURS AND EVENTS TAKE PLACE AT MONTICELLO EACH DAY; PLEASE
CHECK THEIR CALENDAR FOR UPCOMING CELEBRATIONS AND OTHER
HAPPENINGS.

MICHIE TAVERN

Michie Tavern

On the road to Monticello just past Carter's Mountain Orchard, you will find Michie Tavern. William Michie, whose family hailed from Aberdeenshire, Scotland, established it in 1784. The Michie family owned the tavern for more than 150 years. During the 1920s preservation movement, Josephine Henderson moved the tavern in 1927 from Earlysville seventeen miles to its current location. Her efforts saved the historic landmark from decay and made it more accessible to the public.

Taverns were considered a way station in the good old days; weary travelers would stop to eat, rest, and then continue on their journey. Michie Tavern was the setting for many political debates, drinking, dining, dancing, and discourse. Today, like their eighteenth-century counterparts, travelers can enjoy a respite from the road. Guests can partake in hearty midday fare, roam through the original rooms of the old Michie Tavern, and soak in an abundance of history and hospitality (Conte 2016).

Taking a cue from history, this tavern was also a favorite of Andrew Jackson, James Madison, James Monroe, and, of course, Thomas Jefferson—who lived practically next door. It also houses a collection of many historical artifacts, such as pieces of prerevolution furniture. In the Keeping Hall, visitors can find William Michie's own rifle hanging on the wall.

There are three floors within the tavern. These floors house many rooms, including a grand ballroom (Taylor 1992). On the first floor, there is a community room where guests could socialize, play card games, or catch up on the latest news. The sleeping quarters were across the hall, where four beds could fit comfortably. If you didn't arrive in time to get a bed, you could always take a space on the floor. In the back of the tavern, there is a kitchen and dining area. The kitchen was brought inside in the 1800s. This room was added to facilitate warmer meals and a larger eating area. There is a .69-caliber gun hanging on the right wall of the kitchen that belongs to the many generations of the Michie family. A china cabinet can be found on the right wall that is very strange at first glance: the shelves are notched on each side. This allowed women to reach up to the high shelves to obtain needed items (Miss May 2016).

As you head up the steep and narrow stairs, you arrive in the Grand Ballroom, which leads to a family bedroom off to the right on the second floor. The Virginia Reel dance was a crowd favorite during this time (Sincock 1992). It is this room where many say they have heard a great celebration happening, with sounds of partying, glasses clinking, and much laughter and merriment. When someone investigates, there is no one in the room (Taylor 1992).

A psychic who visited the tavern and ballroom stated she felt many people around in a jovial mood and dancing. She thought the ballroom was used only on

Michie Tavern Ballroom

specific occasions; this particular happening was an anniversary. She felt both Alexander Hamilton and Thomas Jefferson as being present at some time, and she saw a woman with brown hair in a long dress. She also picked up on another man in very fancy dress, who she thought was the woman's husband. The couple had just come to have fun at the evening's festivities. The man was identified later as John Walker. His father owned Castle Hill (Holzer 1997, Holzer 1998).

Back in the 1930s, Milton Grigg and his wife owned the tavern. They divorced, and Mrs. Grigg stayed at the tavern. She used to complain about not being able to sleep at night because of all the commotion and activity that was occurring in the ballroom and other parts of the tavern.

The curator for the museum, Cindy, used to be a long-distance runner. Despite her endurance, climbing the steps to the ballroom could leave her out of breath. Several other hostesses were also athletic, and they too were so short of breath that they had difficulty talking about the upstairs rooms to touring guests. Cindy said there was a heaviness in the ballroom; at the end of the day, all the hostesses would compare notes about their experiences. There was never any consistency though. Some days were normal with no occurrences. Other days, the hostesses were so winded they could barely talk (Conte 2016).

When you finish your tour and are ready to eat, head to the Ordinary. Their lunch buffet is five star and served family style. Beware when you step into the dining room that is straight past the serving line and up the stairs. There have been reports of dark spots in the peripheral vision that may give you chills.

More recently, a hostess was getting ready to begin the day shift and stopped in the women's bathroom in this same dining room. She saw a woman with a tan cape enter the restroom before her. When she walked in, she heard the door to the handicapped stall bounce closed, like someone opened it and just didn't lock it. The hostess took the other stall. When she came out, she washed her hands and prepared to go back out and greet the first visitors. She thought it was eerily quiet in the bathroom all of a sudden. She knocked on the handicapped stall door and asked if the woman was all right. There was no answer. Thinking the woman may be ill, she peeked under the door and did not see any feet or legs. She stood back up and opened the door to find no one was in the stall (Conte 2016).

One little boy, who was having lunch with his father, stated he saw a ghost in the men's bathroom. He also said the ghost was a bad man who had been in jail for a while.

The curator told about one morning when she was in the kitchen making coffee, and there were a stack of plates leaning against some trays. No one else was in the building except two other kitchen workers. Suddenly, the top plate went flying across the room. Startled, she asked what happened. The two kitchen workers stated this was a usual occurrence in the kitchen—a plate or dessert bowl would just fly off the shelf.

In the front room of the Ordinary, many people have heard footsteps around midnight. If you listen, you can hear heavy footfalls across the threshold of the front

Michie Tavern Front Room

door. No one hears the door open, but the steps sound as if someone wearing boots enters the building and slowly walks down the hall.

Once you have eaten, head down the hill to the General Store, where you might see another spectral visitor. It is also known as the Meadow Run Grist Mill and is recognizable by its two large waterwheels both inside and outside the building. There is a spirit that the hostesses have labeled as "He." After the General Store is closed, they can hear him walking upstairs as well as opening and closing cabinets (Taylor 1992). There is a story of an alarmed tourist claiming she saw an apparition. As an employee tried to reassure the frantic guest, several books flew off the shelf and landed right next to them (Conte 2016).

The curator also mentioned two very distressed women in the backroom of the gift shop. She walked back to see if they were all right, and they were both staring at a candle lying on the floor. They told her that the candle had flown off the table and across the room and then abruptly fell to the floor. They were deeply startled by the incident.

The last story concerns a paranormal team investigating hauntings at the tavern. There was an intense thunderstorm, which made conditions ripe for ghostly activity. Microphones and cameras were stationed throughout the old tavern. The paranormal group seemed to find success in attracting a wandering spirit. Through questioning, the entity indicated he was from France. The investigators kept telling this ghost that if he answered one more question, they would leave the tavern. However, they didn't; they continued to prod the ghost with question after question. Suddenly, they heard restless pacing in the backroom. Once the team began packing their equipment, the pacing stopped. Prior to leaving, they stood by the staircase, which led into the backroom. Group members

Michie Tavern General Store

were saying their goodbyes when they heard heavy footfalls leave the backroom and ascend the stairs. The footsteps paused for a moment on the landing, within inches of the paranormal team, before continuing up the steps to the ballroom. The team literally tripped over one another trying to escape the tavern. The lesson learned was never to lie to the spirits (Conte 2016).

MICHIE TAVERN
683 Thomas Jefferson Parkway
Charlottesville, VA 22902
434-977-1234
www.michietavern.com
Stop and have an old-fashioned lunch with all the fixings and check out the ballroom and General Store. You may have a couple more in your party than you originally thought. There are also several shops to enjoy as well: the Clothier Shop, the Metal Smith Shop, and the Armory.

Mount Eagle Farm

As you drive down Route 53 (Thomas Jefferson Parkway), you will miss this particular farm if you aren't careful. It is hidden quite well, and there is just a small driveway and a sign on a tree letting you know you have found it. The farm is a private residence, so do not go exploring without permission. Albemarle County is in the process of protecting this farm from having any more developments (O'Bryant 2016).

Built in the 1770s for Lucy Jefferson by her husband, Colonel Charles Lewis, the house was first known as Monteagle. Lucy, being Thomas Jefferson's sister, wanted to have a large home. Not only does this particular domicile have twelve rooms, but the property it is located on boasted 1,500 acres of land that sat beside the Rivanna River.

According to owners, there has been much activity in the house that they simply cannot explain by normal methods. There are reports of cabinets opening and closing, someone walking through the house, and apparitions that appear from nowhere and disappear just as quickly. One owner stated she saw a man standing over her baby's crib. When her husband tried to speak to the man, he vanished. The current owner states that she feels a presence in the house at certain times (Baars 2016).

There have also been other occurrences that are unexplained. Several times, a man has been spotted that they think is their grandfather going for a drink of alcohol, since the plantation had a moonshine distillery on the grounds (Twisted Paranormal Society 2015a). There have also been disturbances in the basement and on the second floor of the mansion, including footsteps and lights flickering (Baars 2016).

There is a graveyard on the property, and one of the headstones is that of a three-year-old girl named AnnieLizzie who was born in 1875 and died in 1878. A brick wall cordons off the cemetery from the rest of the property.

Does this little one have anything to do with the mischief that occurs in the house? After much research, I could not find any information about the young girl except for what was on her gravestone (Baars 2016).

MOUNT EAGLE FARM
PRIVATE RESIDENCE

ASH LAWN–HIGHLAND

While Jefferson had Monticello and Madison had Montpelier, James Monroe, fifth president of the United States, moved to Highland. It consisted of a tobacco farm that spanned 540 acres of the property. Monroe's wife, Elizabeth, changed the name to Ash Lawn. They lived in the home for over twenty years with the exception of when the Monroes resided in the White House. Monroe's house is only three miles from Monticello, owned by his good friend Thomas Jefferson.

Ash Lawn was considered a modest home when it was being constructed. Monroe, in much debt at the time, still erected a two-story addition in 1860. With 3,500 acres for the house and grounds, the farm produced tobacco and wheat for the Monroe family. Around 1974, the house and grounds were left to the College of William and Mary.

In April 2016, the foundation was located, showing where Monroe's original house stood before it burned down sometime before 1870. The house on the property at present was actually the guesthouse (white; attached to back of main house) along

Ash Lawn–Highland

with part of the original (yellow). The large white oak tree, which stands to the right as one exits the front door, has been dated at over 300 years old and thus was present when Monroe lived on the grounds (Preston 2011).

There has been much speculation about a certain happening in the house. A chair rocks back and forth by itself. All the owners after Monroe claim to have seen the chair rocking in the main room of the house when no one was around it. If someone touched the chair while it was rocking, it would immediately stop (Holzer 1997).

Many thought it was Monroe himself. He is said to have sat in the rocker after retiring at night. Could he be watching over his beloved home?

Another theory about the mysterious chair tells of a small girl who lived in the home after Monroe's time. She had hung her hair over the back of the chair to let the flames from the fireplace help dry it faster. Her hair wound up catching fire, and she burned to death. It is said that her cries can still be heard in that room by the fireplace.

We may never discover the identity of the rocking-chair ghost. When asked about this occurrence, most tour guides for Ash Lawn will say they have never heard of the chair. It was taken from the home many years ago and placed in storage. Does it still rock on there? Does the little girl still cry out for help? One can only hope she has finally found peace (Taylor 1992).

ASH LAWN–HIGHLAND
2050 JAMES MONROE PARKWAY
CHARLOTTESVILLE, VA 22902
434-293-8000
WWW.ASHLAWNHIGHLAND.ORG

THERE ARE SEVERAL TOURS TO
CHOOSE WHEN YOU VISIT THIS
HISTORIC HOME; CHECK THE WEBSITE
FOR CONTACT INFORMATION AND
MORE DETAILS.

TANDEM FRIENDS SCHOOL

Tandem Friends School front entrance

Founded in 1970, Tandem Friends School is a much-needed alternative to the current teaching methods. They are diverse in their programs, dedicated to the arts (drama, art, and music), and require community service for all students in addition to their studies. The school enrolls grades 5–12. Currently, they are serving approximately 240 students (Tandem Friends 2016). There are three buildings on the property: the two-story, white mansion-like school, and two smaller red-brick buildings beside it.

The older building is said to have been a location for a Civil War hospital for wounded soldiers. Many apparitions seen in this building are still covered in blood. In addition, there are footsteps heard on the upper level along with the anguished moans of those who were hurt (*Blue Ridge Gazette* 2006).

One student stated that he saw some strange things while he was a student at Tandem Friends School. Several students decided to camp out in the attic one night and saw a little boy who used to live in the attic. He also reports a Confederate soldier walking the halls, which everyone from the principal and teachers to students have witnessed (Strange USA 2008).

Other occurrences at the school include unexplained footsteps, water faucets turning on by themselves, and doors opening on their own. Some people believe the specter is William Farish, who built the structure around the 1840s. It is speculated that he and some other family members, roughly twenty of them, are buried either near or under where the current school is located. This may or may not be true, but as construction on one of the newer wings commenced, a casket was found containing a woman dressed in period clothing (Puccio 2005).

TANDEM FRIENDS SCHOOL
279 TANDEM LANE

CHARLOTTESVILLE, VA 22903
434-296-1303
WWW.TANDEMFS.ORG

CARRSGROVE MANSION

Built in 1748, Carrsgrove was constructed mostly of stones rather than brick or wood (Hauck 2002). It is a two-story home with one-story wings on both ends of the mansion. Both James Monroe and Aaron Burr lived in the mansion. Some nails and one door have been dated back to 1760. The current owners are descendants of Aaron Burr, and they decided to call it "Carrsgrove" after acquiring it in 1955 (City of Charlottesville 1977).

On December 28, 1978, the furnace system malfunctioned, causing a fire when the Burr family was at home. Flames were seen on the first floor and in a second-floor bedroom. Many antiques and other family heirlooms were destroyed, but no one was certain of the complete damage done (Granger 1978).

A mother is said to haunt one of the bedrooms on the second floor. She thought her daughter had cholera and was going to die. The mother took poison so she wouldn't have to go on living without her. The little girl lived, but the mother passed away. Sobbing is heard in the hallways near the bedroom (Hauck 2002).

CARRSGROVE MANSION
192 STRIBLING AVENUE
CHARLOTTESVILLE, VA 22902
PRIVATE RESIDENCE

UNIVERSITY OF VIRGINIA

The University of Virginia (UVA) started in 1800. Thomas Jefferson had decided that a new college was vital in the Old Dominion because William and Mary did not have enough courses in the sciences, and he wanted a university closer to the center of the state (Thomas Jefferson Monticello 2011). The land where UVA is located was purchased by James Monroe in 1788. The first classes began in March 1825. Where other institutions allowed only three specialties (religion, medicine, and law), UVA allowed many different specialties, such as philosophy, architecture, political science, and astronomy. Thomas Jefferson was known as the guiding light to UVA and its legacy. At one point, Jefferson wanted to ban theology, saying it had no place within the institutional walls. Today, however, UVA does have an ongoing Religious Studies specialty, which includes a nondenominational chapel on the grounds.

In 1817, the first stone of Pavilion VII was laid as Thomas Jefferson surveyed the site and decided to start building his university. By 1821, at least six of the pavilions would be finished. The university officially opened on March 7, 1825.

In 1826, James Madison, who served as the fourth president of the United States, became rector of UVA. James Monroe, the fifth president, lived on the grounds at Monroe Hill and stayed there until his death some years later. Thomas Jefferson also visited the grounds one last time in June before his death on July 4.

Alderman Library

The year 1826 also brought Edgar Allan Poe to the university. His room on the West Range is still maintained by the Raven Society, and it has a short audio recording telling all about Poe and his achievements at UVA. Poe also attended Sunday dinners with Jefferson at Monticello for new students.

Edwin Alderman became the university's first president in 1904. The Alderman Library is named in his honor. Alderman brought many reforms to the school that helped with financial needs of the students. He was considered ahead of his time and served twenty-six years at UVA.

President Franklin Roosevelt visited the university in June 1940 to see his son, Franklin Jr., graduate. In 1957, William Faulkner joined UVA as its writer-in-residence. He was a professor of English and kept office hours until he died in 1962. Martin Luther King and other civil rights leaders also spoke at the university in the early 1960s. Queen Elizabeth II walked the grounds and had lunch in the Rotunda's Dome Room in 1976. The Dalai Lama visited the grounds for a week, attending the Nobel Laureates conference in 1998 (Thomas Jefferson Monticello 2011).

UVA has a rich history and is filled with people who have made many changes in the world today. It sits in the center of the state, as Jefferson wanted, and it still brings a sense of pride to Virginians who are alumni or just starting their educational journey. The grounds are one of the most beautiful in the world.

There are many sites to view at UVA, but you must visit the Academical Village (Great Lawn, Rotunda, and Pavilions), the Alderman Library, Poe's Room on the West Range, the UVA Cemetery at Alderman and McCormick Roads, and what is known as "Stiff Hall." All of these offer something to the ghost hunter in all of us. They all have interesting tales that accompany the beautiful façade of each building.

THE ROTUNDA AND THE ALDERMAN LIBRARY

Heading down University Avenue, the first building you should notice at the north end of the Lawn is the Rotunda. It mimics the Pantheon in Rome, including the dome at the top, which also housed one of the original libraries. It burned down in 1895 and was properly restored in 1976. Dr. Bennett Wood Green, who died in 1913, left a large portion of his book collection to UVA's library. This collection was originally in the Rotunda library. His ghost, known to haunt this particular room, would check on his collection and ensure the library staff was taking proper care of it (Powell 2014).

When his books were moved to the new Alderman Library in 1938, he accompanied them. There are unexplained footsteps, and some of the staff have felt like someone or something was watching them, especially if they are in the library after midnight. One staff member who has encountered Dr. Green's ghost started bringing her dog with her while working (Powell 2014).

Rotunda and Great Lawn

President Casteen's office in the Alderman Library

The Alderman library also claims another ghost in their midst. This spirit is known to haunt the Garnett Room, which is now President Casteen's office. The room houses many books donated by Muscoe Russell Hunter Garnett's family. This ghost is believed to be an old family physician who used to make house calls when the Garnett family lived in Fredericksburg. After the estate was abandoned, the doctor's spirit took care of the book collection that was gifted to the Alderman Library. The doctor still stands watch over the collection (Viccellio 2012).

THE LAWN

It is considered a distinct honor to live in one of the Lawn Pavilion rooms the final year of education at UVA. There are at least fifty-four rooms located where Thomas Jefferson had built part of the school originally. There is no air conditioning in any of them, but they each have a fireplace within a 12-by-13-foot room.

There is a story attached to the Lawn dating back to the mid-1800s. A professor of UVA died, and his wife decided she wanted to keep living in their home located on the Lawn. To accomplish this, she placed her husband's corpse by the window in the apartment every day. She made people think he was still alive, since she changed his clothes daily as well. When his death was finally discovered, she was promptly asked to leave the property (University of Virginia 2016).

PAVILION VI

Pavilion VI

This building is also known as the Romance Pavilion, since there is a tragic love story attached to it. In the late 1800s, a professor's daughter fell in love with another student. Her parents did not approve of the relationship, and this caused a rift between the girl and her boyfriend. They broke up, and the girl eventually died of a broken heart. It is said that her ghost still haunts the pavilion looking for love.

The real reason for the building being called the Romance Pavilion is because many of the Romance languages are taught there. These includes Spanish, French, Italian, and Latin (Viccellio 2012).

PAVILION X

When Edward Younger, a history professor, taught at UVA from 1946 to 1974, he lived in Pavilion X with his wife. His mother-in-law came to visit and stayed on the ground floor of the Pavilion in the back. Something awoke her one night, so she looked around to see who was in the room, thinking her daughter had come in while she was asleep. She discovered a man dressed in 1800s clothing beside the bed, staring down at her. She was not the only person who saw this apparition. Another history professor as well as Professor Younger's nephew both claimed to have seen the ghost in the room or on the staircase. When the nephew called for help, the man vanished (Rathbone 2013).

Pavilion X

POE'S ROOM ON THE WEST RANGE

Edgar Allan Poe, one of the greatest writers and poets of his time, attended UVA from February to December 1826. He couldn't continue further with his studies because his father wouldn't give him sufficient funding. To meet some of his expenses, he started gambling to keep up with his debts. But he was unable to meet his expenses, and he left the school at the end of the December term.

Poe entertained his peers and professors by reading his tales and his poetry to them. One tale he wrote, "The Tale of the Ragged Mountain," is supposedly written about the Charlottesville mountain range. The Raven Society, established in 1904, keeps room 13 on the West Range furnished with pieces of the time. They were not Poe's, but they do resemble the furniture in his room when he attended UVA. Poe had to break up his furniture for firewood to keep warm during the winter. He went to UVA with hardly any money to help support him, and yet, he still went on to become a best-known writer (Kelly 2011).

Before he left in December 1826, he left a mysterious message etched in one of the windowpanes of his room. It speaks of "the ghost of an awful crime" (Viccellio 2012). Did he see a ghost in room 13? Was he working on another poem for reading? No one could ever figure out exactly what it meant, and it is still puzzling to this day.

STIFF HALL

When you ask students at UVA where Stiff Hall is, they just look at you and say they have never heard of it. I asked several people when I visited the grounds; however, no one could tell me where it was located. Stiff Hall is located behind Peabody Hall, where the north wing of Newcomb Hall currently sits. This nickname was given to the Anatomical Laboratory, where human dissections take place for those in medical programs. Stiff Hall came about because one of Thomas Jefferson's physicians had gotten upset that the bodies were kept on the first floor of Pavilion X. Jefferson understood what the physician meant, and built another theater for the purpose of dissection. Reports from students and faculty state strange smells and sounds coming from the room, as well as lights being on after they were turned off for the night (Barefoot 2010).

UVA CEMETERY

UVA Cemetery entrance

Located near the corner of Alderman and McCormick Roads, this cemetery is divided into two different sections: the Confederate and University. There are roughly 1,100 Confederate soldiers buried here, as well as two canine mascots of UVA, Beta and Seal. In the University section, the first person buried was Dr. William Henry Tucker in 1828 (Cooper 2007). Many doctors, lawyers, politicians, and alumni from UVA are also buried in the University section.

The site was plagued by grave robbing in 1828 and the years that followed. Bodies were taken because laws forbade any dissection or possession of human remains. Relatives took to burying their loved ones after dark to save them from being disturbed by the robbers, although the robberies stopped after Virginia passed another law that allowed medical schools to legally obtain bodies for dissection (Maurer 2008).

UVA CONCLUSION

UVA has become a hot spot for paranormal research. They have recently opened a new Division of Perceptual Studies, researching reincarnation and near-death experiences, and work with many children who remember living a past life. They also investigate out-of-body experiences and how they happen. The Perceptual Studies web page is https://med.virginia.edu/perceptual-studies. You will find a completely new world waiting for you, and some very interesting research.

UNIVERSITY OF VIRGINIA
160 MCCORMICK ROAD
CHARLOTTESVILLE, VA 22904
434-924-0311
WWW.VIRGINIA.EDU/

TRAX NIGHT CLUB

Trax Night Club was so named because it was located off West Main Street near the railroad tracks. It was widely known for being one of the first venues for the Dave Matthews Band in Charlottesville. Opening in 1982 and closing around 2001, a developer reopened it in late 2001 under a different name. The University of Virginia was the last known holder of the property. They tore it down in 2002 and placed the UVA Medical Center in its place (Jaquith 2002).

The nightclub's employees experienced many strange and unusual happenings while working there. Some would notice the occurrences after they had locked the doors for the night and returned the following morning. Lockers and coolers would be open when workers closed them before they went home. Furniture was constantly rearranged, and all the faucets would be turned on full blast. There was a young girl, Little Suzie, who wore her hair in pigtails, and many employees, including the manager and bartenders, saw her in a green dress. She appeared inside the front door and immediately told people the club was closed. No one could discern if her feet were actually touching the floor as she moved. The manager followed her to the front door and she vanished.

There were also reports of people moving around in the upstairs area, but when checked, the door was locked and no one was in the room (Jaquith 2002).

There have been no reports of anything unusual at the UVA Medical Center that is now sitting where Trax used to be.

TRAX NIGHT CLUB
11TH STREET NEAR UVA HOSPITAL
DEMOLISHED IN 2002

CASPARI

Caspari entrance off Downtown Mall

Caspari first opened in Paris in 2001 at Rue Jacob. The Charlottesville store opened its doors in 2005. The products within the store are inspired by many different collections of the world, including private collections, the Royal Horticultural Society, and the National Gallery in Williamsburg, Virginia. They offer items to dress up any occasion from a dinner party to a wedding. You can find linen napkins, jewelry, picture frames, and candles (Caspari 2016).

Before Caspari moved to the corner storefront, Woolworth's had a store in the location for around forty years. Edward Perely owned it before Woolworth's, and he ran a funeral parlor in the 1960s.

After Woolworth's moved in, there were some upsets among the employees. Coffins from the funeral home were left behind in the basement. This made the lower floor more spooky. There were also noises heard that no one could explain, such as where they were coming from or how they were made (Rathbone 2013).

I spoke with the woman who owns Caspari today, and she stated they had not seen or heard anything unusual since they had been in the location.

CASPARI
100 WEST MAIN STREET (DOWNTOWN MALL)
CHARLOTTESVILLE, VA 22902
434-817-7880
WWW.CASPARIONLINE.COM

INN AT COURT SQUARE

Front door of the inn

The Inn at Court Square is well known by its bright-red door. It has a total of five rooms, some having a fireplace for keeping the guests warm in the winter. Built in 1785 by Edward Butler, this inn is one of the oldest buildings in Charlottesville. In 1808, the house was sold to Opie Norris. It became known as the Butler-Norris House (Nunley and Elliott 2004). Many businesses have originated here, such as a slate company, a law firm, a church, and real estate brokers. The inside of the building has many examples of eighteenth-century woodwork and architecture (Rathbone 2013).

There are many ghost stories that have evolved at the inn. One concerns a porter, John, who carried the guests' luggage up to their rooms. A three-candle sconce hung on the wall at the bottom of the staircase. Every time John took the luggage upstairs, he would knock the sconce off the wall. He requested they move it somewhere else, but the owners left the sconce where it was. John died a short while later, and after his funeral, weird incidents started to occur. Many guests noticed water dripping in the area where the sconce was located. Later that year, the owner felt something fly past her. When she looked on the floor, she saw a candle from the sconce. No one else was near the stairs or the sconce (Rathbone 2013).

I spoke to Candace DeLoach, who currently owns the inn, and she told me a couple of different stories. She verified the story of the candle falling out and rolling across the floor. This occurred the day after John passed away. One year after John's death, water began running from the same spot again. Candace found a plumber to fix the issue. He discovered that some nails holding the sconce had pushed into a water pipe and punctured it. These nails had been in the wall for two years. It was as if something pushed the nail farther in just to cause more issues. Candace placed the eulogy she read at John's funeral in the wall before the plumber closed it. They have not had any more issues. The sconce itself is no longer at the inn, which has since been sold (DeLoach 2016).

Other guests have spotted a lady in an upstairs room wearing a hat and period clothing. Another guest saw a doctor in historical military dress standing beside her bed one night. When she screamed, he disappeared (DeLoach 2016).

Did John finally find peace? It seems like he did. It also seems he invited a few friends to visit with him.

Location of candle sconce on stairs. *Courtesy of Steve Allen*

INN AT COURT SQUARE
410 EAST JEFFERSON STREET
CHARLOTTESVILLE, VA 22902
434-295-2800
WWW.INNATCOURTSQUARE.COM

OLD ALBEMARLE COUNTY JAIL

Built in 1876, the jail with its surrounding property was the fifth constructed in Albemarle. Erected from the stones of a previous jailhouse located over on Court House Square (Albemarle County Old Jail Museum 2014), the jail remained open until 1974 to house inmates and other criminals (Jones 2016).

Surrounding counties sent their most dangerous inmates here. The walls are three feet thick and made of solid rock. Bars cover all the windows; the doors are made of heavy metal, and they are very hard to open and close. They did have special slots in the doors for meals to be served to each inmate. The jailer lived right beside the facility, and his wife would cook the many meals for the inmates. These meals consisted of fried pork, beans, and black coffee. Prisoners didn't receive dinner unless they worked outside the jail, such as on a road crew. Two prisoners would occupy each cell; however, by the 1970s, that number could go up to four.

Today, visitors go down four steps to get to the front entrance of the jail, which consists of two white, half-moon-shaped doors. Once inside, a breezeway leads to the jail facility in the back. In the old days, the road came straight up to the white doors, and wagons could travel into the jail to pick up or drop off prisoners, depending on their destination. The interesting thing about the breezeway is its wooden ceiling. It has held up for over 100 years (Jones 2016).

As you make your way to the jail, you see a huge metal door that is locked. I asked Paul (our tour guide) about any of the prisoners escaping from this facility. He stated that if the inmates managed to get out of their cell, they had to get through two heavy doors (a cell door and a fire door) and the front gate before they could be free. Interestingly enough, the outside wall of the jail is white. When an inmate was left outside by mistake, he would show up against the white wall. The inmates did not wear specific uniforms; most wore the clothes that they had on upon entering the facility. They had a small sink and shower on the bottom floor where they could wash out their clothes by hand if necessary.

Breezeway through front of jail

The cells on the second floor housed the women prisoners. One of the more famous inmates, Samuel McCue, was on the second floor in the right corner. People were imprisoned here for any number of offenses, such as stealing, gambling on Sundays, drinking in restricted areas, and murder. Unfortunately, the second floor is not accessible because the stairs are not in good shape.

The jail was also the hanging site of Samuel McCue, the former mayor of Charlottesville, in February 1905. McCue was accused of murdering his wife, Fannie, in September 1904. He was forty-five years old and was a very successful attorney who worked with domestic cases and collection of debts. There were rumors he was cheating on Fannie for many years. Since he was a very cantankerous man who disliked the poor, people were ready to convict him when he became the main suspect for the murder. Although many people found discrepancies between the testimony and the actual timeline of the crime, McCue was hanged in the gallows on February 10, 1905. It took almost twenty minutes for him to succumb from the hanging. He left behind three children and several close family members (Gribben n.d.). (See the section on Comyn Hall for the complete history of Sam McCue and the murder that tore his family apart.)

Upon entering the jail and its surrounding buildings, I began to feel a chill. As I walked through each cell, I could feel some of the anguish that went on here. I can describe it only as a weird and unsettling feeling. I felt a heavy depression along with cold chills throughout the buildings.

When asked about any unusual or strange happenings within the jail itself, Paul told us of several instances when he discovered he wasn't quite alone. During the

Jail cell with two beds; you can almost feel the despair.

spirit walks they do every fall, last fall brought a strange occurrence. Paul was playing a jailer character, and he sat in the pitch dark with just a lantern in the breezeway area waiting for the next tour to arrive. It was late October, so the leaves were falling and strewn across the walkways. He heard a sound like someone walking beside the jail through the leaves. He took his lantern and walked around the corner to see if it was someone from the next tour, and there was no one there. A few minutes later, he heard the footsteps again as clear as day. He initially thought it was someone from the historical society playing a prank on him. He decided to sneak up behind them and get them first. He walked completely around the jail, but no one was lurking in the dark. He did keep hearing the footsteps through the leaves for a good long while after that (Jones 2016).

Paul also wrote an article in *The Hook* back in 2003 concerning some happenings and also about the McCue murder (Jones 2003). He relates a story from last summer where he heard haunting footsteps once again. Sitting in a chair in the breezeway, he was waiting to show people around the jail buildings on a Saturday. The breezeway has a concrete floor and is about five to six feet long. All of a sudden, he started to hear someone with hard shoes walking across the concrete. When he turned to see who it was, no one was there. These incidents occur mostly in the courtyard, but this particular happening occurred in the entrance itself (Jones 2016).

OLD ALBEMARLE COUNTY JAIL
409 EAST HIGH STREET
CHARLOTTESVILLE, VIRGINIA 22902
WWW.VISITCHARLOTTESVILLE.ORG/EVENT/OLD-ALBEMARLE-COUNTY-JAIL-TOURS/14181/

Comyn Hall entrance and face in upper window

COMYN HALL

Comyn Hall is well known in Charlottesville. It is the location of the murder of Fannie McCue, wife of Sam McCue, the mayor of Charlottesville in 1904. Sam originally built the house and named it after a mansion on Park Street that had been demolished. In 1929, the house was converted into a retirement home and renamed the Walter-Dickinson Home. They changed it back to Comyn Hall in 1967. An addition was added in 1970 to the right side of the house. The retirement home closed in 2008, and in 2009 an estate sale took place to remove the rest of the furnishings, including the bathtub where Fannie McCue died, located in the basement (Earnst n.d.). Today, Comyn Hall advertises twelve residential apartments complete with modern fixtures (Woodard Properties 2011).

What really happened the night of the murder? No one truly knows, but there are several versions of the story. They all end with Fannie McCue being found dead in her bathtub from a gunshot wound to the chest. She had also been stabbed and strangled (Oyster Ranch 2011).

In his book *The Hanging of Mayor McCue* (Jones 2005), Paul Jones brings up some good facts disputing what had previously been known and testified to in court. On September 4, 1904, Sam and Fannie headed to church services down the road. Sam had to return to the house, so Fannie went on alone to the church. This was a strike against Sam, since they had not been seen arriving together. They left the church around 9:00 p.m., after the services were finished, and they bade goodbye to their friends. They arrived home about fifteen minutes later.

As they started to enter the front yard, they saw Marshall Dinwiddie, Sam's uncle, and spoke with him for a few minutes. He testified they both seemed relaxed and even invited him to chat, but he had to be getting home himself. Both Sam and Fannie entered the home straightaway after bidding his uncle good night.

Staircase where Samuel McCue was found by his brother, Frank

Across the street, two neighbors were watching the whole situation play out. Mr. and Mrs. Frank Massie both wondered why they were retiring this early in the evening. It was only around 9:15 p.m. Fifteen minutes later, Mr. Massie saw Sam's brother, Frank McCue, enter the house. These fifteen minutes between when the McCues entered their home and when Frank showed up are clouded in mystery.

Out of the McCues' four children, only Willie, the sixteen-year-old, was at home. He had left earlier to see a friend, and he would be returning soon. The theory was that Sam killed Fannie during those fifteen minutes. When Sam told his version, it was very different. He stated that an attacker had been in his bedroom. He was hit on the right side of his face, knocking him unconscious. After he woke up a few minutes later, he called for help saying Fannie had been shot, and he had been attacked by an intruder.

Sam finally reached his brother, Frank, who arrived at 9:30 p.m. Frank found Sam sitting on the stairs looking confused. When he saw his brother, he urged him to check on Fannie. Frank took the steps up to the second floor and heard the bathwater running. He found Fannie in the tub, with no pulse. Sam approached a few minutes later only to fall down and sob at hearing about Fannie's demise (Jones 2003).

The next day, Sam did some things that looked strange for a man who killed his wife. Not only did he offer $100,000 for information leading to the arrest of the killer, he also hired a detective to assist in solving the case. Unfortunately, the only murderer found by the detective was Sam himself.

Many witness accounts describe a man going down the front stairs and around the corner of the house after the attack transpired, but no one ever followed up on this lead. There was much circumstantial evidence involved in the trial; however, the prosecution used it to their advantage. There were several inconsistencies in all the eyewitness accounts. These were never pursued. Some witnesses changed their testimony over the weeks leading up to the trial as well.

The final ruling was that Sam had killed Fannie after a bitter argument after they entered the house. He shot, stabbed, and strangled her and injured himself in the face all in the time frame of fifteen minutes before calling for help. Jones refers to the fact that someone else was waiting in one of the upstairs bedrooms to end Fannie's life after she saw them come home together. According to Jones's

Fannie McCue gravesite and space to the left for Samuel, although her name is the only one on the stone.

book, it was not a man that killed Fannie; it was a woman named Hattie Marshall. Sam had been seeing her for a while, and she finally decided to take what she wanted (Jones 2005).

Since she saw Sam walk to the church on his own that night, she assumed he would be back after services, and they could be together. She thought Fannie was out of town that weekend. As fate would have it, both Sam and Fannie arrived home and went straight to their bedroom to retire for the evening. Hattie, who was hiding in their daughter Ruby's room, attacked Fannie with a fireplace poker as she walked by, which almost took her ear completely off. It did succeed in knocking her to the floor. Hattie turned to go back to Sam and saw he had the shotgun from his closet ready. She hit him hard in the face, and he fell over to the floor, recognizing her at the last second. Hattie then took the shotgun with her to the bathroom. She shot Fannie in the chest directly. The bullet ripped through her aorta and broke three ribs.

A few minutes after the shots were fired and Frank had shown up at the house, the neighbor, Mr. Massie, noticed a male with a light-colored hat and dark clothes run down the road and toward town. Jones states that the male was actually Hattie Marshall disguised so no one would know it was her. Many eyewitnesses talked of another person being in the house besides Sam and Fannie. All these accounts went unheard or unnoticed by the court.

After the trial, the jury took approximately twenty minutes to decide that Sam was the guilty party. He was sentenced to hanging on January 20, 1905, and was executed three weeks later, on February 10. He was buried at his parent's home but in 1907 was moved to Riverview Cemetery to rest beside Fannie. Only her name is on the stone, but he is right there beside her (Jones 2005).

It is said that Sam and Fannie still haunt the home where their lives were forever changed. Fannie haunts the upstairs bathroom, and Sam haunts the basement area. Their bedroom has also been a site for many strange occurrences. Maybe when the truth is finally known, both Sam and Fannie can finally rest in peace.

COMYN HALL
601 PARK STREET
CHARLOTTESVILLE, VA 22902
PRIVATE RESIDENCE

Dunlora Mansion

The Dunlora Mansion has been part of Charlottesville's history since 1730. It started out as a farming plantation; the same family owned both the land and estate (Cairns 2016). Known as one of the oldest homes in Charlottesville, it is located in the woods at the end of a lengthy road (McKendry 2016a). As a result, it is not easily seen from the road or surrounding properties.

As with all old properties and plantations, there is a story that goes along with the mansion. The story involves six murdered boy scouts and their scout leader (Kelly 2016). This was the first time the scout leader had taken the troop camping, and he wanted to make sure it turned out to be a nice trip. He did not know about the stories or the rumors that still existed regarding the witch on the property (McKendry 2016a). Apparently, he went looking for his scouts at a campground near the Dunlora Mansion. Many campers who knew the story of the land and property were careful never to set foot on either (McKendry 2016a). A witch who lived on the grounds in the early 1900s was accused by the scout leader of killing the six scouts by slitting their stomachs open. After police investigated the crime, they questioned the leader and, after hearing his version of events, immediately classified him as a lunatic. He was arrested for the murders and committed to an insane asylum for the rest of his life, where he couldn't harm anyone else. The damning evidence: the police found the scout leader's knife, covered in blood, in a log next to the campfire.

The spirits of the boys are said to still inhabit the property, particularly the trees at the entrance of the property. The scout leader is also said to roam the property and the crooked and twisted tree up front (Kelly 2016).

Other strange occurrences keep the rumors alive to this day. One person said he used to live in the house cleaner quarters near the main house. He heard footsteps and had the feeling that someone was watching him at the same time. He noticed that the motion sensor would go off with each footstep down the hallway. He also said a few graveyards were located on the estate and could be downright creepy at times (Ghosts of America n.d.b).

Another inquisitive person made a trip to find the Dunlora Mansion, and they were scared out of their wits. They drove down the dirt road leading to the house just fine. When they got ready to leave, the car started having all kinds of issues. The engine didn't run properly, all the electronic devices in the car were going crazy, and the radio continually looked for a station but never seemed to find one. Once they reached Rio Road, the car drove perfectly (Ghosts of America n.d.a).

Several teenagers out for some kicks decided to check out the mansion just to see if the stories were true. They noticed that along the dirt road to the house there were eight trees. When they drove back out, they counted only seven. They decided to stop in the middle of the dirt road, roll down the windows, and listen to see if they could hear any unusual noises. They didn't have to wait too long as they immediately heard the sound of several little boys screaming. They rolled the windows up and got out there as fast as possible (Ghosts of America n.d.c).

Are these stories fact or fiction? The caretaker for the Dunlora Mansion stated he has worked on the property for years and has never witnessed anything strange or unusual. He stated that many people trespass on the privately owned residence in hopes of seeing something supernatural. He asks that everyone please respect the owner's privacy (Cairns 2016).

DUNLORA MANSION
PRIVATE RESIDENCE
DO NOT TRESPASS

MAPLEWOOD CEMETERY

When entering this beautiful cemetery, you see many ornate and older obelisks marking the graves. Many of these graves are from the 1800s and, notably, the Civil War. This tour is rich with the history of Charlottesville and its people. This was the first public cemetery in Charlottesville, having been around since 1827. Many Confederate soldiers and officers, as well as soldiers who were Freemasons, are buried here instead of in the UVA Cemetery. There are no plots left; however, if you can prove you're related to someone who has empty lots, you may be buried here

Looking across Maplewood Cemetery

alongside the family member (Kutch 2016). There are also more than one hundred unmarked graves within the cemetery walls (City of Charlottesville 2016b).

The imagery and language used on gravestones have also changed over the years. They used a carving of death's head back in the 1800s. Today, they may use carvings of urns or willow trees to show death and its meanings. The language that was used reflected the time, since they would say "Asleep in the Lord" or call someone the "Wife of X" (Kates 2011).

There are also some African Americans buried in Maplewood, along with many slaves who lived with specific families. One stone for an enslaved woman named Hagar is inscribed with "Faithful Servant." She is buried near the Meade family plot, suggesting that she may have served them. No death date is given (Rainville 2011). There is another woman named Linie Winston, who also has a gravestone marked with "A Faithful Servant," but unfortunately there is no other identifying information on her stone (City of Charlottesville 2016b).

The first gravesite you see is that of Letitia Shelby, who was the first governor of Kentucky. She died suddenly in 1777 while visiting Charlottesville.

Thomas Wood died in 1895, and he was the mayor of Charlottesville at the start of the Civil War. He was also the oldest member of the legal bar.

William McLeod Abell was shot and killed at twenty-two years of age while in the 5th Virginia Calvary.

Paul Goodloe McIntire died in 1952. He donated many parcels of land to Charlottesville for park development.

John Bowie Strange, a colonel in the Confederate army, was killed in the Battle of Boonsboro in 1862. He was in the 19th Virginia infantry.

John Marshall Jones, a brigadier general, died in 1864 at age forty-three at the Battle of the Wilderness. He also fought at the Battle at Gettysburg.

Mosby Parsons, a brigadier general in the Civil War, died in 1865 at forty-three. He was also a district attorney in Missouri (Kutch 2016).

Richard Thomas Walker Duke, also known as RTW Duke, died in 1898 at age seventy-six. He was a Confederate colonel in the Civil War. He was also a member of the House of Delegates and assigned to be the commonwealth attorney in Albemarle, Virginia (Library of Virginia n.d.).

Maud Coleman Woods, the first Miss America, lies beside her parents in a cradle grave. She died at twenty-four from typhoid fever in Hanover County in 1901. She had her picture taken as part of a sitting with a photographer who entered the pictures into a competition and actually won. The pictures were released in a book by Alexander Black titled *Miss America: Pen and Camera Sketches of the American Girl* (New York: C. Scribner's Sons, 1898).

Maud's father, Micajah Woods, was a commonwealth attorney who assisted with Sam McCue's murder trial in 1904. He also served in the Civil War and became 1st lieutenant in 1863.

Richard Omohundro, who owned the Exchange Hotel in Gordonsville, is also buried here. One of his bartenders, Reuben Morris, was laid to rest beside him. He slipped on a corncob in a barn and was killed.

One of the more interesting people in the cemetery is Louis Brown. He was a headstone carver, yet he has no stone marking his burial site.

Left: Gravesite of Hagar, identified as "faithful servant"

Right: Gravesite of Maud Coleman Woods, the first Miss America

Another cute story about the graveyard's inhabitants concerns three sisters. One married and lived into her forties. The other two sisters never married and lived well into their hundreds. Wonder what this means?

Wilson Cary Nicholas Randolph was a great-grandson of Thomas Jefferson. He studied medicine at UVA and was a surgeon for the Confederate army during the Civil War. He was also UVA's rector for eight years.

Margaret Hunter Rion, who died in 1862, was a nurse and matron of Midway Hospital, which was part of UVA Hospital at the time. When she died, many of her patients followed the hearse to the church to pay their last respects (Kutch 2016).

Benjamin Franklin Ficklin, who was a cofounder of the Pony Express and died in 1871 after choking on a fish bone, is buried here as well (City of Charlottesville 2016b).

These are just a few of the stones you will come across at Maplewood Cemetery. They were doctors, lawyers, nurses, and soldiers. They even have one Miss America. People of all classes and occupations are buried here, some in family plots.

As you go through Maplewood, you will discover that many of the metal pieces are missing from the fences. This is due in part to a metal drive during World War II. There is also an African American section on the right side of the Maple Street entrance. A sad sight in the cemetery is that many of the gravestones have fallen over time. Others may have been removed because they had broken into several

A strange mist in the trees at Maplewood Cemetery

pieces and needed to be repaired. Most are the original stones of the people who are buried there. Maplewood has no discernible walkways or sidewalks, and the headstones are arranged in a haphazard manner throughout the grounds. It has only a brick wall surrounding the perimeter.

As we made our way through the grounds, I noticed the quiet and serenity of the grounds. This cemetery is filled with so much history, especially from the Civil War. You can definitely feel the ghosts of the past coming back to tell you how they lived and died.

There is a report of seeing a figure walking through the graveyard at dusk. When someone went to find the figure at the gate, the figure had vanished. There have also been assorted noises heard throughout the cemetery. I photographed a mist over one of the graves while I was there. It is definitely worth a trip to see if you have a unique experience as well.

MAPLEWOOD CEMETERY
425 MAPLE STREET
CHARLOTTESVILLE, VA 22902
434-970-3260
HTTP://STOWEKELLER.COM/PORTFOLIO/CITYPARKS/CEMETERIES/
MAPLEWOODCEMETERY_HOME.HTML
OPEN FROM DAWN TO DUSK

THE FARM
(LEWIS FARM)

The Farm, also known as the Lewis Farm, is a historic home that belonged to Nicholas and Mary Lewis. She was the daughter of Thomas Walker, who owned Castle Hill. Nicholas Meriwether owned the 1,020-acre property in 1735. A professor at the University of Virginia acquired a piece of the estate in 1825. He had workers from Thomas Jefferson's Monticello build him a house, using architecture specific to Jefferson himself (City of Charlottesville 2016a). Only the cook's house is still standing on East Jefferson today. There is a British soldier and Lewis descendants buried on the grounds. They are in unmarked graves; however, the soldier is said to be buried on a hill overlooking the Rivanna River (Long 2005).

The house is rich with history, and perhaps the most notable occurrence is what happened on June 14, 1781. Colonel Banastre Tarleton stayed overnight at the Farm. Tarleton spent the night by the fireplace while American prisoners of war were thrown in the cellar for the night.

The next morning when Tarleton and his men were getting ready to leave, they took everything that they could carry. This included all of the Lewises' food and farm animals. They even snatched all of Mary's ducks except for one lone drake. Mary figured they had taken all the other animals and ducks, so they may as well have this one. She sent an enslaved girl to catch up with them and deliver the drake. Tarleton took the drake and dispatched the girl back home to deliver his gratitude to the Lewises (Long 2005).

Many people now get feelings of despair and uneasiness when they go near the fireplace (Hauck 2002). Does the ghost of Colonel Banastre Tarleton still linger in front of the fireplace, or is it the British soldier looking for peace?

THE FARM
1201 EAST JEFFERSON STREET
CHARLOTTESVILLE, VA 22902
PRIVATE RESIDENCE

SILVER THATCH INN

Quaint and rustic with charm, the Silver Thatch Inn is a bed and breakfast that will make you wish you had a longer vacation. It is off Route 29 in Charlottesville, not far from Fashion Square. It is set back in a quiet neighborhood and has many amenities that everyone can enjoy. It comes complete with seven rooms and an outside pool; each room is named after an early American president born in the state of Virginia. The inn is located in the heart of Charlottesville, not far from many other attractions, such as Monticello, Ash Lawn–Highland, and Skyline Drive.

The property started out in 1780 as a barracks for Hessian soldiers who were captured during the American Revolutionary War by General Horatio Gage. The structure, built on an old Indian reservation, served as a jail for the captured soldiers

Front of Silver Thatch Inn

(Nunley and Elliott 2004). Several wings were added to the inn between 1912 and 1937. The land was used as a tobacco and melon farm, while the inn itself was used as a school for boys (BBOnline.com 2016).

B. F. D. Runk, dean of the University of Virginia, owned the inn in 1937 and added an additional wing to the house. The property stood until 1983, when a married couple developed a full-service bed and breakfast. They decided to call it Hollymead Inn due to the location.

Today, it is owned by Jim and Terri Petrovits and known as the Silver Thatch Inn. They have kept to the standard of helping their visitors get away from it all— there are no televisions or phones in any of the guest rooms. Breakfast is served at individual tables. Dinner is also offered at the inn to the guests as well as to the public (Nunley and Elliott 2004).

After speaking with Terri for just a few minutes, I surmised that this bed and breakfast had all the amenities needed to have a great vacation and not worry about the outside world. They also have had their share of paranormal activity around the cottages. Don't ask to be placed in one of the units, though. The owners will not tell you which one is haunted.

One of the most notable occurrences is that sometimes a Hessian soldier will playfully steal a guest's pillows during the night. You will wake up with no pillows anywhere (Nunley and Elliott 2004). Voices are heard on the lower level, and there is a story about an entity going upstairs and sitting in a chair with a loud sigh. A guest just happened to be in her bathroom when this occurred. She heard the floor squeaking with each step. When she opened the door to see if her husband had returned, she quickly discovered that no one else was in the room (Cooking Light 2004).

The Jefferson Room has had its share of occurrences as well, since it is in one of the older sections, dating back to 1812. There is a family cemetery somewhere on the grounds. One guest told the owners she felt a very strong presence in the inn, but she felt that it was a good entity and quite friendly. A man and his wife also stayed in the Jefferson Room and were treated to a ghostly visitor. He woke up around 4:00 a.m. and saw an apparition move from one side of the room to the other. He watched it for a while and went back to sleep a little while later, not frightened of the entity (Cooking Light 2004).

SILVER THATCH INN
3001 HOLLYMEAD DRIVE
CHARLOTTESVILLE, VA 22911
434-978-4686
WWW.SILVERTHATCH.COM
GORGEOUS WEEKEND GETAWAY AND VACATION SPOT LOCATED MINUTES
FROM CHARLOTTESVILLE'S MAJOR ATTRACTIONS AND SHOPPING OUTLETS.

WICKHAM FARMHOUSE

The Wickham Farmhouse was built by Richard Durrette in 1781. The current owner acquired the residence in 1951. She has had several occurrences while living in the farmhouse, ranging from noises to footsteps and apparitions (HauntedHouses 2016).

Mary W. discovered that when the fireplace had been remodeled, around 1938, an inscription was found on the wall. It told the story of how prisoners of Hessian soldiers assisted in building the chimney in 1781. The rest of the house consists of a main room, a hallway, and a bedroom that can be reached only by staircase. It is the older part of the farmhouse that seems to have the spiritual activity.

One night while she was in another part of the house, Mary W. heard what sounded like people moving around in the main room of the home. She heard them moving back and forth across the floor, as well as swishing sounds that may have come from dresses or riding clothes. She thought it was a family member who had forgotten to tell her they were back. She called out to her family but received no answer.

She made her way to the main room to see what was happening. On her way, she passed a window that looks out toward the barn some thirty feet away, and she saw her entire family standing outside the structure. It couldn't possibly have been any of them who made the noises. When she reached the main room, she saw no one.

When her two daughters lived at home, Mary W. and her husband would entertain guests on the property at another cottage nearby. On one of these occasions, the girls were in their rooms upstairs when they noticed what sounded like people walking around downstairs at 10:00 p.m. They thought for sure it was their parents or maybe one of the other guests. When they asked their parents about it the next day, both said that no one had left the party all night.

Psychic Virginia Cloud visited the house to discern why the spirits were there. She saw a man in a nice shirt and pants with boots, but he was dragging himself around in the room. Was he an injured soldier or landowner who was caught in the crossfire? He also seemed to be calling to his mother, who had died many years previous.

The ghostly footsteps are thought to be Mary W.'s husband, who died in the house. He also had the same foot-tapping motion and restless movements as the ghost that haunted his bedroom (Holzer 1997).

WICKHAM FARMHOUSE
PRIVATE RESIDENCE

TALLWOOD

Tallwood was owned by the Coles family, who built it from 1804 to 1834. It is near Enniscorthy, which is the third Coles plantation, and the estate joined Enniscorthy and Estouteville as family homes in Albemarle County (Mucci 2015). Tucker Cole, one of the original builders, married Helen Skipwith. Wanting to improve upon the "small" house, Helen set to redecorate and add to its charm after she inherited money from her mother. Tallwood was originally developed from the Enniscorthy estate (Taylor 1992).

In 1840, a Native American burial ground was found on the property. After receiving special permission, the Native Americans danced around the site in honor of the dead buried there (De Alba 1993). There has never been another gathering such as this since that time.

The grounds are filled with English yew trees, which are helping solidify its ghostly stories and atmosphere. The magnificent home boasts twelve rooms and a spectacular garden area filled with lilacs, crepe myrtles, and other gorgeous foliage. Helen took some time developing the gardens the way she wanted, making them a beautiful addition to the property (Taylor 1992).

A descendant of the Coles family tells about the occurrences at the house. On November 7, 1789, there were ten children living in the house. The older two, Peyton and Selina, had already gone to live elsewhere. A maid hurried out of Peyton's room and refused to clean any longer because she had seen a gun on the shaving dresser, and she was deathly afraid of them. Selina, unfazed by the gun, said she would go and retrieve it from the room. Suddenly, a gunshot was heard. When everyone entered the room, Selina was lying on the floor, dead from a gunshot wound. Everybody immediately thought it was an accident because Selina knew how to handle guns expertly.

Now, as it turns out, on the seventh of November every year, the window in the room opens by itself and a cool breeze engulfs the room. Most of the family will not even go in the room on that particular date (Taylor 1992).

TALLWOOD
PRIVATE RESIDENCE
THE MANSION IS NOT ABLE TO BE SEEN FROM THE ROAD.

SUNNY BANK

Being a landmark, Sunny Bank has been added to the National Register of Historic Homes. It sits near the South Garden area in Albemarle County. Built in 1797, Sunny Bank is a two-story home with the wings added over a twenty-year period. There are other structures on the property, including a laundry facility, smokehouse for meats, and a log shed. A family cemetery sits just behind the house (United States Department of the Interior 1976).

The historic mansion is also home to two ghostly women. They first made themselves known in the early 1900s by moving furniture and making footstep noises throughout the house. Sinks would sound like they were beginning to fill. Perhaps the most fun was in 1920, when the two women started materializing in front of the owners. They both appeared in the bedrooms where they'd perished. The ghosts are thought to be Betty Dew and Constance Cazenove. They are related to the Hart family, who have owned Sunny Bank for the last 200 years (Hauck 2002).

Mrs. Hart awoke to find a young woman sitting on the edge of her bed. The woman was believed to be Betty Dew. Another guest spotted a young woman in front of a mirror, combing her long blonde hair. Constance Cazenove had returned to the room where she died (Taylor 1992).

The psychic manifestations continued to get more and more bold. These include chairs rocking in empty rooms, sounds of a horse and carriage coming up the drive, and more unexplained footsteps through the home (Taylor 1992).

According to L. B. Taylor (Taylor 1992), there was a third apparition in the house. This apparition took the form of an older woman. She liked to walk through doors in the mansion; the doors were locked at all times. They would shake every so often, and the owners would know she wanted to go outside.

SUNNY BANK
PRIVATE RESIDENCE

2.

GREENE/MADISON/ CULPEPER

GREENE

Lafayette Bed and Breakfast

LAFAYETTE INN

This quaint little bed and breakfast in Stanardsville serves some great dishes, and the ice cream is the best in town. When we were visiting, there were about five or six people in line to try the frozen delight.

Declared a historic landmark, it is a three-story building with a dining room on the lower level. Built in a federalist style, the house has a wraparound porch and large windows for one to enjoy the majestic views. All the rooms provide the best accommodations; some even have a fireplace to boot. The innkeepers, Alan and Kaye, traveled for many years before settling down in Stanardsville to open their unique inn. They had different ideas as to what would make a place inviting and welcoming to their guests. They decided to put all those ideas to work for them when opening the Lafayette. They have five rooms named after presidents. They also have the Dicey Cottage, which accommodates four people and is named after an enslaved man who lived in the cottage during his life (Our Roots 2017).

The original quarters for the slaves can be located at the edge of the property. Most guests can enter the building by the second floor, built in 1840. Behind the main building is an annex that used to be a stable, which housed a small kitchen area and an office. Other businesses also thrived in the same location, such as a saloon, restaurant, and hospital during the Civil War. During the war, General Richard S. Ewell came to Greene County after being ordered by General Stonewall Jackson. There were 8,500 men who came through town; some had contracted typhoid fever and stayed in available buildings. The Lafayette Inn was likely one of the locations (Our Roots 2017).

Some unusual events have occurred over the years. There is a bloodstain in the foyer under a corner of one rug. This bloodstain reappears every morning no matter how hard it was scrubbed the previous night. The blood is from a Confederate soldier who killed himself after learning of his wife's unfaithfulness. He still roams the halls of the inn with his pistol ready to kill the Yankee soldier who had an affair with his wife (Kinney 2009).

LAFAYETTE INN
146 MAIN STREET
STANARDSVILLE, VA 22973
434-985-6345
WWW.THELAFAYETTE.COM

BLUE RIDGE POTTERY

The Blue Ridge Pottery specializes in gorgeous pieces of handmade pottery and stoneware. The main building to the right of the pottery may have been a place for weary travelers to stay after riding all day. The building dates back to 1827 and has served as a military headquarters, a restaurant, a hospital, a motorcycle shop, and an inn (Journey through Hallowed Ground 2017). The pottery has been in residence since the 1980s, selling porcelain products and high-fired stoneware. Each piece takes six to eight weeks to be completed (Blue Ridge Pottery 2015). The building stood vacant for many years because no one showed any interest due to its history (Taylor 2010).

The owner doesn't like to speak about the ghostly presence in the main building. There is a legend concerning several murders within the main house, although the number can range from seven to seventeen (Taylor 2010). One occurred because two men were having a gunfight on the stairs. The property owner murdered some of the others so she could steal all their possessions (Foam Cage 2010).

One of the members of the Historical Society for Greene County was visiting and felt that someone was following her around the shop. She was very cold on a

Blue Ridge Pottery Wedding Building

hot summer day, and there was no one else present. She was also in the room where a card player may have been shot. Another writer heard that there was a bloodstain at the foot of the stairs, similar to the Lafayette Bed and Breakfast, that cannot be removed. He also told a story about a little girl who likes to roam the shop and main house. Some visitors can see tiny handprints after she visits (Foam Cage 2010).

The owner was quoted in the local paper as saying that he thought the ghosts were just mischievous. He tries to talk to them and keep them happy. One time when he was working at the shop alone, he heard sounds upstairs like people were moving furniture around. The location was used as a Civil War hospital, and many soldiers have been seen at the top of the stairs. There is also a story about a soldier and some gold on the property. The soldier was killed and never told his wife where the gold was hidden. Sometimes, a soldier is seen roaming the halls. Perhaps he is looking for his lost gold (Taylor 2010).

BLUE RIDGE POTTERY
9 GOLDEN HORSESHOE ROAD
STANARDSVILLE, VA 22973
434-409-3319
WWW.BLUERIDGEPOTTERY.COM

MADISON

EAGLE HOUSE

Eagle House

Eagle House is listed in the county records as far back as 1804. William Carpenter owned the house then, and he had the property deeded to his sons upon his death. The current structure on the property was built in 1832. In the original building, a tavern was incorporated, as an eighteenth-century walnut bar was located in the basement. From 1833 to 1957, there was a long history of people who deeded the property to family and friends. Mrs. Philip Morrison purchased the home in 1957 and set to work completely refurbishing and restoring the home to its former grandeur (Dove 1975).

The three-story house was built in many sections and has a fireplace in every room. A flowing staircase enhances the main entrance hall. The house also has an east addition and an L-shaped wing. The walnut bar in the basement served as a model when Colonial Williamsburg was doing their restorations. During its days as a tavern, the home welcomed many weary travelers from the Blue Ridge Turnpike traveling both in stagecoaches and carriages. It is thought that both George Washington and J. E. B. Stuart visited the tavern for refreshment when traveling, but no proof has been uncovered to prove this (Dove 1975).

One tragedy occurred around 1827. A teacher spanked one of his students for an offense he'd committed. The student's father became angry and shot the teacher. He was arrested and sentenced to hang. On the day of his hanging, there was a huge festival in Madison, since most of the townspeople had shown up to witness the hanging. The mood was very solemn throughout the crowd. As the time approached for hanging, an unsettling darkness fell over the town. Many thought it was divine intervention because God was angry. The darkness dissipated by evening, and the hanging took place as scheduled (Dove 1975).

EAGLE HOUSE
201 NORTH MAIN STREET
MADISON, VA 22727
FOR INFORMATION, CALL MADISON COUNTY HISTORICAL SOCIETY AT
540-948-5488.

HUNTON HOUSE

Hunton House Hotel

Built in 1802 by Alexander Hunton, the home had three stories and no front porch at the time of completion. The porches were added in 1849 to make the property more welcoming. Located at the north end of Main Street, the home became the Hunton House Hotel with a kitchen addition (Dove 1975).

The early 1900s brought electricity and indoor plumbing to the hotel. The only problem was the water tower, which stood only a few feet taller than the hotel. When people used the restroom or took a shower, the water pressure was dreadfully low. In the 1930s, the town finally placed their own water lines and didn't allow the use of wells. People who owned the hotel had a pit behind the building, which ran the hotel for many years until the Hunton family decided to employ the town water lines.

Unfortunately, in 1919, a horrendous fire took out most of the buildings on Main Street. Sarah Hunton Hall was in possession of the hotel at the time. After the fire was extinguished, it took much rebuilding to restore the town and the hotel to its former glory. The new three-story addition had several rooms on the first floor, a library on the second floor, and twelve rooms on the third floor (Madison County Historical Society 2010). It also had a ballroom, which still looks the same, and thirteen bedrooms. Sarah Francis Johnston, mayor of Madison, was the last person to own the property (Breeden 2016).

There are several ghostly occurrences at the hotel today. There is a chest of drawers that cracks every so often. The unnerving issue is that right before a family member dies, there is a loud noise that sounds like a gun being fired. Many people have been invited to look at the chest, but they have no explanation as to what is causing the noise. It does not happen with extreme temperatures, but only before a family member dies (Dove 1975).

Another story concerns a ghost that roams the property. This apparition appears when the hotel is changing hands or if there is a huge crisis in the family. Usually found on the second-floor porch, the door will open like someone is walking through it (Dove 1975).

HUNTON HOUSE HOTEL
211 NORTH MAIN STREET
MADISON, VA 22727
FOR INFORMATION, CALL MADISON COUNTY HISTORICAL SOCIETY AT
540-948-5488.

THE GEORGE H. LEITCH HOUSE

Standing on the west side of Main Street, the original house on what is now known as George H. Leitch House property was built in 1799. Research from 1834 references the lawsuit of Jones versus Jones, which states that the house was then in heavy disrepair. Records from 1840 show that the house no longer stood on the property. George Leitch bought the property in 1853 and constructed the current house.

The home was built with two chimneys and a brick basement. The three-story home also contains six fireplaces, two on each floor. With each addition, the rectangular home formed into more of an "L" shape. Rebuilding one of the porches as a kitchen in the 1950s allowed the family to gather in a larger dining room (Dove 1975).

When Dr. and Mrs. Powell were living in the house, they had an amusing occurrence. Many noises kept them awake at night after moving into their new residence. The sound came from outside their bedroom door, sounding like someone was walking back and forth. The Powells knew the story of Terle Taylor, who had

The George H. Leitch House

a peg leg and loved to walk the halls when he was living there. They figured the loud banging was the peg leg as it hit the wooden floor. After some research and observing, they found several turkeys had roosted near the roof, and they found out that Terle Taylor did not have a peg leg (Dove 1975). Were the turkeys making the loud noises, or was something else?

THE GEORGE H. LEITCH HOME
311 NORTH MAIN STREET
MADISON, VA 22727
FOR INFORMATION, CALL MADISON COUNTY HISTORICAL SOCIETY AT
540-948-5488.

THE THOMAS W. WELCH HOUSE
(KEMPER RESIDENCE)

Located on the north end of Madison, this fifty-two-acre site is currently owned by the University of Virginia (UVA). The property has a history of deed transfers since 1833, starting with William Twyman. Thomas Welch acquired the land in 1852 and started building his home between 1852 and 1857 (Dove 1975).

Perhaps the most well-known tenant was James Kemper, the thirty-seventh governor of Virginia from 1874 to 1878. He also served as a Confederate general in the Civil War and suffered from wounds received at Pickett's Charge. He retired to his estate in Orange County, Walnut Hills, where he died on April 7, 1895, and was later buried on the property (Madison County Historical Society n.d.).

The Thomas W. Welch Home (Kemper Residence)

The three-story structure contains an English basement, two fireplaces, and eight large columns. The columns support the front porch with an Ionic persuasion on the ground level. The third floor incorporates high ceilings and fireplaces with decorated mantels. Outside are two smaller buildings; the smallest was employed as a law office for James Kemper (Dove 1975).

The home is continually being restored. The Madison County Historical Society is refurbishing the home with furniture and clothing from the time period. UVA is the current owner, and they use the home for classrooms.

Culpeper Paranormal Investigations visited the site and collected some evidence of a haunting at the location. They heard voices on their recorders, asking who they were and actually calling one of the investigators by name. The investigators took many pictures in which they found orbs to be present. They thought this might have been the entity trying to show itself in their photo (McKenna 2016).

THE THOMAS W. WELCH HOUSE (KEMPER RESIDENCE)
414 North Main Street
Madison, VA 22727
For information, call Madison County Historical Society at
540-948-5488.

OLD JOHN FISHBACK HOUSE
The interesting thing about this home is that it is no longer standing. A new residence resides just down from the original but now-torn-down house on the property. Martha Breeden owns the property and is a descendant of the Fishback family

(Breeden 2016). I also believe that she is related to me, since I have Breedens in my family tree as well, including an aunt named Martha Breeden who passed away in the 1980s.

The family came from Germany and had six children. One of their grandchildren, John, built the Fishback Home in the 1790s. The house sat on one hundred acres given to him by his father. John and his wife, Anna Clore, raised twelve children on the property. Children, grandchildren, and great-grandchildren lived on the property until 1948, when Mrs. Ashby Fishback inherited fourteen acres from her husband upon his passing (Dove 1975).

Each cornerstone of the house, which sat one mile east of Madison, faced a different direction. It came with two fireplaces and a very steep roof. The second floor had two bedrooms, and the entrance to the basement level was beneath the front porch, where rocks lined the walkway down to rooms with dirt floors. In 1939, another bedroom was added. Outside, there are two graveyards on the property near the north wing of the house. One of these graveyards was for slaves and holds twenty-two graves, and the other holds twelve Fishback relatives (Dove 1975).

John Fishback was employed as a wheelwright. He made most of the wagons that traveled through town heading to their next stop (Breeden 2016). One of the finest-equipped shops at the time, John's wheelwright shop employed a treadmill and the assistance of oxen and horses. Many of the older homes in Madison were built with nails and hinges that John made in his wheelwright shop (Dove 1975).

Some Civil War soldiers came upon the house and made it their campground. They ate most of the chickens, pigs, and wheat products. There was nothing left in the house, because when the family saw the soldiers coming, they burned all their valuable pieces (Dove 1975).

It seems the wife of Robert Edward Lee Fishback, Gracie Maud Weaver (grandmother to Martha Breeden), complained of seeing a ghost in their home. She would try to arouse her husband whenever the ghost appeared, but he never saw it. He asked her to describe the entity, and although Gracie had never seen his father, Staunton Fishback, she gave him a perfect description of the man (Breeden 2016). It is thought that Staunton hangs around to monitor his beautiful home (Mills 2000).

THE OLD JOHN FISHBACK HOME
No longer standing
For information, call Madison County Historical Society at
540-948-5488.

THE OLD CAPTAIN ANDREW CARPENTER HOUSE

This particular home is still standing today. Located south of Brightwood on Route 629, Jean Dixon is the current owner and another relative of Martha Breeden's great-grandmother (Breeden 2016). The date of construction of the house, which was originally owned by Captain Andrew Carpenter, is unknown. There is some history between the Fishback and the Carpenter families; there is also a Crigler family mentioned as the ownership is traced backward (Dove 1975).

The structure itself is made of log and employs fireplaces on the first floor. The enclosed stairs on the second floor are near two bedrooms in the original section. The addition to the house is separated from the main house by a hallway that runs between them.

The house is said to be haunted by Mrs. Marc Wayland (nicknamed "Pus"). After Pus died at her children's home in Roanoke, horrible sounds were heard on the second floor. At first, it seemed that someone was walking back and forth. The sound grew increasingly louder, sounding like a cane going across the roof shingles. When someone checked the upstairs, nothing was out of place (Dove 1975). Also occurring on that same night: she appeared at the Carpenter House even though she died ninety-six miles away (Mills 2000).

THE OLD CAPTAIN ANDREW CARPENTER HOME
PRIVATE RESIDENCE
FOR INFORMATION, CALL MADISON COUNTY HISTORICAL SOCIETY AT
540-948-5488.

THE RICHARD BLANKENBAKER HOUSE

Located on Route 609 near Haywood, the home was occupied by Richard Utz Blankenbaker during the mid-1800s. In 1850, Richard lived in the Carpenter Tavern, which later became known as the Eagle House. The Blankenbaker House is currently owned by Mrs. Earl Fitzgerald (Dove 1975).

Facing south with the most-gorgeous views of the valley, the two-story house has a basement, two floors, and an attic. When the Blankenbakers owned it, they added a porch, a bathroom, a kitchen, and a dining room. The springhouse behind the home is the original structure (Dove 1975).

As far as ghostly happenings are concerned, Mrs. Tanner remembers the time she saw something out of the ordinary. She was on her way to supper when she passed her parents' bedroom. Out of their window, she saw a woman in a gray ruffled dress walking in the yard. Thinking that she was a visitor whom no one had heard knock on the door, Mrs. Tanner leaned out the window to tell her to come back; however, she no longer saw the woman. She ran outside with her brother, who also searched and found no one else on the property. The woman in gray has been seen numerous times over the years. Some people think it is Sarah Blankenbaker, but there have also been reports that the entity was much taller and thinner than Sarah was in her lifetime (Dove 1975).

An older member of the cooking staff also claims to have seen the ghost. She was preparing some chicken for a church meeting, and on her way to the hen house, she heard the gate open behind her and lock closed. She figured it was the wind and thought nothing of it until she approached the house. In the front porch chair, she saw Sarah Blankenbaker rocking back and forth. As she started to take a closer look, Sarah vanished.

Another owner has seen the shoes of the ghost coming from the bathroom and walking into the dining room. They sounded like the shoes were a soft leather, and it happened in the older part of the home.

THE RICHARD BLANKENBAKER HOME
PRIVATE RESIDENCE
FOR INFORMATION, CALL MADISON COUNTY HISTORICAL SOCIETY AT 540-948-5488.

LOVELL

This gorgeous plantation is one mile north of the post office in Locust Dale. The property was known as Terrell Land, named after the original owner, John Terrell, in 1803. His daughter, Ellen, inherited the house and renamed it Lovell (Dove 1975).

Made of brick with a sloping roof, the house contains twelve rooms and plenty of high ceilings throughout the structure. A covered brick path leads to the kitchen down in the basement. There is also an original fireplace, fully restored, that measures six feet by six feet (Dove 1975).

Two graveyards are present on the property, both of which contain members of the Lovell family. One is in a field near the house, and the other sits on a hill overlooking a nearby river. These have led to many ghostly tales. One is about a headless ghost that roams the flat area near the house, usually during howling winds. The story behind this ghost dates back to the Civil War, when Yankee soldiers came looking for food. The cook told them there was no food left, since soldiers who had visited earlier had taken it all. One soldier decided the cook was lying and searched the kitchen thoroughly. He found a root cellar with meats and other items. As he started to retrieve the items, the cook came up from behind and beheaded him. She then buried him under one of the coffee trees in the yard. He still roams the property waving his arm around and searching for his head (Mills 2000).

LOVELL
441 LOVELL DRIVE
LOCUST DALE, VA 22948
FOR INFORMATION, CALL MADISON COUNTY HISTORICAL SOCIETY AT 540-948-5488.

THOROUGHFARE MOUNTAIN FARM

Located southwest of Leon out on Route 631, the property was owned by William and Mourning Bickers in 1831. The Bickers family stayed until 1891, when they deeded the property to the Garnett family. It has been owned by the Sisk family since 1934.

The farmhouse has two different sections, with the south side of the building being the oldest. Constructed with logs, it shows the workmanship of the time with a stone chimney and an attic. The home boasts high ceilings and a stone foundation. There is also a graveyard in the front with many stone markers, where some soldiers killed during the Battle of Cedar Mountain are buried. One stone is that of a twelve-year-old boy named Anthony Garnett (1889–1901). There could be more Garnett family members buried on the land, but it is unknown if they are (Dove 1975).

Thoroughfare also has a headless-horse ghost that gallops and runs into the barn. Some of the farmers make sure to check that all the horses are in their stalls. An accurate count is always obtained so they are left to wonder about this phantom horse. Could it be one that belonged to a soldier who is buried on the property? The Aylor family, who lived on the property at one time, reported seeing a Confederate soldier riding a headless horse. These horses, with and without riders, were frequently seen running up the driveway and vanishing into thin air (Mills 2000).

Another ghost story concerns a child crying in the basement. There is an old story about a family who lived in the house at some point and starved their young child. His hunger cries are still heard at times (Dove 1975).

THOROUGHFARE MOUNTAIN FARM
PRIVATE RESIDENCE
FOR INFORMATION, CALL MADISON COUNTY HISTORICAL SOCIETY AT
540-948-5488.

OTHER MADISON HOMES

There are other Madison homes that have paranormal activity. These are certainly not all the haunted homes in Madison, but those listed will give you a head start.

Luxmont is owned by the Lights and is south of the Madison Courthouse. A restoration of the home was completed in the summer of 1974. Some of the people who have lived in the house say they felt a presence there. Some spotted a baby in the northwest room window of the third floor at dusk. To make the grounds even spookier, there is a graveyard south of the main house, although there are no ghost stories that accompany it (Dove 1975).

Golden Rock, also known as the Lillard Home, had an original land grant of around 300 acres back in 1734. The home was originally a cabin where slaves lived. This property also went through a complete restoration in 1960. As far as ghostly spirits, one story stands out from the rest. It was hog-killing time one year, so Hiram Lillard started heating water in a pan over a fire in the yard. When he returned to the kitchen to get his hog utensils and instruments, he noticed loud thumping and banging in the back staircase. He made his way toward the kitchen door, and one of the men helping him with the hogs appeared in the doorway. The man stated he had seen Old Lady Lucy. This spirit, believed to be Lucy Collins Richards, lived in the home around 1863. The man refused to spend the night in the house again. The family mused that the fire outside could have caused irregular shapes on the wall . . . or did it (Dove 1975)?

White Oak Hill Farm, located on Route 721, has been in the Weaver family for six generations, having been constructed in 1859. The two-story structure has a stone foundation with chimneys made of brick. There is a folktale about a child named Jim Towles. He was helping some other children pick up wood chips. Someone playfully told him to place his hands on the chopping block. He then lost all but two of his fingers from one chop. It is also said that a bright light shines in the family cemetery the night before a relative dies (Dove 1975).

Edgewood is a mile south of Route 620, and the gorgeous property is owned by the Williams family. It is a two-story antebellum home made of brick and boasts a hanging balcony. It also employs a secret staircase to find a study on the second floor (Dove 1975). It is home to many farm animals, such as goats, horses, cows, and geese, as well as having ponds stocked with native fish (Virginia Estates 2016). People who lived in the home say there is a ghostly presence within the walls. A female roams a bedroom on the second floor. Could it be one of the previous owners making sure her home is watched over now that she is gone (Dove 1975)?

The Reynolds House is another undisclosed location in Madison that exhibits ghostly activity. The house sits where another once stood. The woman who owned the previous house poisoned her whole family, including the dog. The current owner states that furniture moves around quite frequently. Two of the upstairs rockers always end up near the windows, along with the chairs in the kitchen. She has seen shadows move through the home very quickly, and felt a cool breeze when this occurs (Mills 2000). Could it be the murdered victims or the woman who killed her family just looking after her home?

THESE ALL ARE PRIVATE RESIDENCES; PLEASE DO NOT TRESPASS.
FOR INFORMATION, CALL MADISON COUNTY HISTORICAL SOCIETY AT
540-948-5488

CULPEPER

THE GRASS ROOTES RESTAURANT

Main dining area of Grass Rootes

Filled with rustic charm from the wooden tables to the inner décor, Grass Rootes is the place to be on a Friday night in Culpeper. The menu offers something for everyone and a friendly family atmosphere. The owner, Andrew Ferlazzo, gave me a tour and told me about the history of the building.

The property is one of the oldest in Culpeper, dating back to 1765. The location housed many criminals and soldiers both from the Confederate and Union sides during the Civil War. The Yowell Hardware Store took ownership in the early 1900s (Sherman 2017). The name "Yowell" still graces the top of the building.

Andrew took ownership in June 2016, fulfilling a lifelong dream of his to start a restaurant in his hometown. He has been in the restaurant business for more than thirty years, doing cooking apprenticeships throughout Europe and the United States. The head chef, Kevin Scott, is a graduate of L'Academie de Cuisine in Maryland. He also trained under many well-known chefs throughout Virginia. They both love food and inventing creative dishes that bring the patrons back again and again. Since the original bill of sale of the building was to Thomas Reade Rootes, the name Grass Rootes was born. It also encompassed Andrew's dream of offering fresh-farmed food that went straight to the table (Sherman 2017).

My interest was piqued in the restaurant when I saw it the first time on a visit to Culpeper. Sadly, it was not open, and I had to call and chat with the owner to find a good day for both of us to meet. When I finally got in touch with Andrew, one of the first things he mentioned was how big a skeptic he was about specific happenings in the restaurant. He explained different occurrences but stated he had no explanation for how they happened. He figured it was stress and anxiety over trying to get the restaurant going. He has had his tools move to different places, such as two tables over from where he had placed them. He has also heard growling around the front room (Ferlazzo 2016).

He finally reached out to the lady who owned the Hazel River Inn; she told him the history of the property. She suggested several ways to cut down on the occurrences. One was to announce himself, especially in the downstairs bar area where there is a lot of activity, and to show respect to those entities. He states that this has helped, since instead of items being thrown against the wall, he sometimes hears singing.

The lady's bathroom on the first floor has a singing entity. Many employees have heard it. Cups fall over or off the shelf for no apparent reason. Andrew also told me about boxes of coffee that slide across the floor in front of him. The piano in the middle room will play the same five notes by itself. Plates spin in the kitchen, usually three at a time. One night, Andrew and a bartender heard a noise in the kitchen, and they found a plate spinning on a steel table (Ferlazzo 2016).

Many of his coworkers made fun of Andrew when they heard about these happenings. However, they were working on the décor around midnight, and the contractor told him he had heard growling all through the restaurant at least three times. There were no storms going on, and no animals around at the time.

Ghost hunters have investigated the property only to hear laughing and singing and obtain pictures of purple and white orbs that dance around, disappear, and show back up in different spots on video. Most of this activity took place downstairs, in a backroom that has a solid-red floor. The first ghost hunter who visited the restaurant introduced himself to Andrew and headed to the bar. When he did, all the pads in the high chairs flipped over and shot toward the women's bathroom with no explanation.

The building used to house a jail and had tunnels and catacombs all leading under the streets. The tunnels served as a place of solitary confinement for some prisoners. It also functioned as quarantine for those patients who had tuberculosis or yellow fever (Ferlazzo 2016).

On my visit, I took my recorder and camera to see if I could capture anything of interest. When I first arrived, I asked about the bathroom. When listening to the recording, I heard a loud creak that did not happen when I was there. I also kept hearing loud metal clinking, such as bracelets or rings. I was not wearing any that day, and I was alone in the bathroom (or so I thought). At one point in the recording, there is heavy static for about four seconds, sounding like an animal scratching something. Andrew previously told me there was laughing and crying heard in this bathroom.

I met back with Andrew to get some more details, and we decided to head downstairs, where much of the activity occurs. As soon as I reached the bottom of the stairs, I was pulled to a specific spot near the stairs. I don't know if it was what was underneath the floor or something nearby. As I walked farther into the downstairs area, I didn't feel the pull as much. Andrew took time to announce himself to the entities, and I followed suit, telling them my name and why I was there. Andrew had to return back upstairs, so I hung out for a bit, taking some pictures and recording.

The area used to be a downstairs bar to the top restaurant. Currently it is used as a storage area, but it does have a lovely fireplace in the center of the room. I walked through the outer room, but I had no other pulls so I headed back toward the stairs. As I got near the stairs, I was pulled very heavily back to the same spot as before. On the recording, I hear smacking noises that I did not hear while recording. There were sounds coming from upstairs at the time, but these sounded like they were right next to me.

I headed back upstairs to tell Andrew of my experiences. I visited the bathroom again to see if the entity might do something. There is a loud humming or moaning on my recorder at this point.

I began talking with some of the staff while waiting for Andrew. Some told me they were brand new and had not yet had an experience, although they do introduce themselves downstairs like Andrew does to keep the spirits happy. One server told me she was cleaning up after closing, and she heard a loud noise. When she looked over, one of the coffee cups had turned on its side. I reached over to test the cup, and they are very heavy. This cup could not have turned on its own without someone (or something) helping it. It was the only one, she said, out of a stack of about twenty. She also told me of another bartender who heard a noise after closing one night in the kitchen. She went to investigate, and a plate had fallen on the floor. It had not broken but was spinning all by itself. She has also heard of plates that fly out of the middle of the stack for no reason. Another bartender has heard the little girl laughing in the bathroom several times.

Kevin Scott, head chef, has had his share of supernatural happenings. Kevin played football for Illinois State and is not easily frightened. He grabbed Andrew one day and asked what was going on in the restaurant. Kevin had come from downstairs and had seen a shadow shoot down the hall and into the bar. When I asked about his experiences, he stated they were mostly shadows moving around through the room. He states that he can put something down for just a minute, turn around, and it is gone. When he was helping Andrew with painting, he kept feeling like someone was walking up behind him.

Kevin told me a story about the kitchen door they could never get open. He and Andrew tried everything to no avail. One day when everyone came into work, the door was standing open. He also mentioned they hear many things falling, but they never find anything broken or out of place (Scott 2016).

After I spoke with Kevin, I headed back out front to bid Andrew farewell and thank him for the visit. I made another trip to the bathroom just to see if I got anything. This time, I heard the clinking metal sounds again twice on my recording.

I left after speaking with Andrew and headed out the front door to get some pictures of the front of the restaurant. I was very amazed at the audio I recorded. It was a very interesting place indeed.

GRASS ROOTES RESTAURANT
195 EAST DAVIS STREET
CULPEPER, VA 22701
540-764-4229
WWW.GRASSROOTESCULPEPER.COM

BRANDY STATION BATTLEFIELD AND GRAFFITI HOUSE

Graffiti House

The battle that took place on Brandy Station was one of the largest ever fought on American soil. It was also the first battle of the Gettysburg Campaign and known as the Battle of Fleetwood Hill. Taking place on June 9, 1863, both the Union and Confederate soldiers tried to hold their piece of land. Many of them had awoken that morning to the sound of heavy gunfire and the sounds of cannons firing. Numbering around 20,500, the men lost on both sides totaled 1430. Robert E. Lee's son, Rooney, had also been wounded (Civil War Trust 2014a).

There are four major sites to visit at the battlefield: the Federal Army of the Potomac Rebuilds, the Calm before the Storm, Charging the Confederate Guns, and the Confederate Line of Defense at St. James Church. The Battle of Fleetwood

Hill is another site located near the other four. Union soldiers set up winter encampments at these locations from December 1863 to May 1864.

The battlefield was very peaceful and calm when my brother and I visited. Hayfields stretched as far as the eye could see, and the only noise we heard were two airplanes flying overhead. A peaceful place to reflect on those who died, some of whom were brothers and close friends. However, they may have fought on opposite sides. A story survived about two college friends who were on the crew squad at Harvard together: Confederate brigadier general William H. F. Lee and Union lieutenant colonel Charlie Mudge. Lee was wounded at Fleetwood Hill, while Mudge was killed at Gettysburg (Civil War Trust 2014b).

There are not many ghostly activities at this battlefield. One person stated he had heard cannons and guns firing late at night. He thought perhaps the battle was still being fought. Maybe the soldiers were hoping for a different outcome each time.

Many of the wounded were transported to Graffiti House, since it served as the hospital during the war. Located on the eastern end of town, Graffiti House is famous for all of the soldiers' signatures and drawings throughout the building, both upstairs and down. Preceding the Civil War (around 1858), James Barbour owned the house. Since the property is near the railroad, both Union and Confederate troops employed it for supplies and medical help extensively.

To leave their mark, soldiers began writing all over the plaster walls. Today, both floors have many signatures, pictures, and notes written to specific people. The earliest piece of graffiti has been on the wall since August 1862. Thirty-four men's signatures and drawings have been identified so far. More signatures were found in 1993, when the house was being renovated. Some of the sketches include horses, forts, other soldiers, young and older women in period clothing, and civilian men (Brandy Station Foundation 2017). The house is a true collection of history—exhibiting what soldiers went through while they were recuperating or just resting before the next battle.

Graffiti House has a plethora of ghostly activity. One story in particular that I really liked was about Michael Bowman, who was in the 7th Virginia Cavalry. When you go upstairs, his room is to the left. There is a picture of this handsome man right under his signature on the wall. Apparently, he is considered a flirt with the women. As you get to the top of the stairs, you may feel a poke or slight pinch. This is Michael just having fun (Smith 2016). His room was much cooler than the rest of the house even though it is upstairs and the temperature was in the eighties the day I visited.

One of the tour guides, Denise, told me she hated going into the building alone, since it was just too noisy. There are many conversations and talking going on all the time, but nobody is ever found in any of the rooms. Her coworker, Tony, also states he has heard talking within the house. The voices come from soldiers who still may be there, and a little girl named Sally. Sally doesn't like Denise because she smokes. She is thought to be eight or nine and enjoys moving things around a lot (Smith 2016). Sally used to come to the house to have hot chocolate and cookies.

Michael Bowman picture and graffiti wall

The kitchen is where the hospital room is located on the first floor. Sometimes when you enter the building, or that room in particular, you can smell chocolate chip cookies (Smith 2016).

There is also a lady in a beautiful blue dress, Harriet Melinda Stone, who was a prostitute back when her brother owned the home. On this particular day, two women had gotten past the other tour guides and headed upstairs. When they came back, they told Denise it was one of the best tours they ever had. It seemed like the person actually lived during the times she was talking about at the time. All the tour guides just looked at each other, since they didn't know what to say. One of them asked who was giving tours upstairs—the funny part was that no one was up there. They all were downstairs in the gift shop. Another elderly couple upstairs at the same time as the two women never saw the woman in the blue dress (Smith 2016).

Other happenings might include doors opening and shutting by themselves and motion sensors going off, but nothing is ever seen. The owners were also doing some renovation in 1993 and attached some curtain rods to the front windows. They went to retrieve another rod, and when they came back, the rod in the curtain was gone. They finally discovered it in the other corner of the room and had no idea of how it got there (Smith 2016).

Some days, glass is heard crashing upstairs. When Denise went to clean it up, nothing was ever broken. Tony heard voices upstairs one day when he arrived. It sounded like two men chatting about last night's football game, very amiably talking. When he went to see who had gotten past him, he found no one. He has also heard people coming down the stairs and walking across the floor. When he goes to search for the culprit, he never finds anyone (Smith 2016).

Are there soldiers still roaming the battlefield and hospital trying to find a way to get back out there and fight again? Are they making battle plans or plotting strategy upstairs, where no one else can hear or see them?

BRANDY STATION BATTLEFIELD / GRAFFITI HOUSE
BRANDY STATION FOUNDATION
19484 BRANDY ROAD
CULPEPER, VA 22714
540-727-7718
WWW.BRANDYSTATIONFOUNDATION.COM

SALUBRIA MANOR

This is a spectacular location to visit. The home is still in great condition considering that it was built before the American Revolution and has lasted through two earthquakes—which caused still-developing cracks in the outer four walls. Made in the style of German architecture, the house has two chimneys and rustication along the brick walls, which gave the outside walls a textured look. The builders also employed the Flemish brick-bond method when building the outer walls, using one long side of a brick then one short side of a brick (alternating stretchers and headers in each course). The glass panes in the windows are specially made for the house, costing $37,000 each in today's dollars. All the windows have seats below them for relaxing on cool spring days. An interesting fact to note is that only one room has electrical outlets.

Salubria Manor

My tour guide for the day was Lena Scherquist, the property manager. Part of her family from 1852 until 2001, the property was purchased by the Germanna Foundation, which hopes to restore its former look.

Reverend John Thompson built Salubria in 1757. He married Anne Butler Spottswood Thompson, a widow of Lieutenant Governor Alexander Spottswood. She died in 1758 and is buried on the property under an oak tree. Thompson later married Elizabeth Rootes, and they had four children.

Lena's grandfather and Cary Grayson were first cousins. Born at Salubria in 1879, Cary's mother died when he was very young. He became a practicing doctor and served as Woodrow Wilson's physician when Wilson was president of the United States.

George Harrison, not the Beatle, took the position of president of the Federal Reserve in 1928. He financed the rebuilding of the house to make it livable again, after many instances of it being distressed or damaged. However, in the 1920s, the money dried up after he died. He wanted to modernize the home with modern conveniences such as plumbing and electricity.

Today, the Germanna Foundation still owns the property. They hold many weddings, parties, reunions, and tours on the grounds. Their wish is still to restore the house and grounds.

Many ghost stories accompany any tour of Salubria, and Lena did not disappoint me. She had many to tell as we walked through the house and grounds. Speaking of the grounds, there are two graveyards located in the back of the house. Many Graysons and Thompsons are buried at the ancestral home. Lena also stated that many paranormal groups come and spend the night, but they never catch anything significant.

On one tour in February 2016, Lena was showing some members of the Department of Historical Resources around the home. They started upstairs as Lena locked the front door behind them. They surveyed the upper floors and then they headed to the basement. The windows in the house do not open; they all are tightly shut. While they were in the basement looking around, all of them heard a door slam upstairs. After checking in all the rooms, nothing was found that would have made the noise.

A lady also killed herself in the home. She stands with a candle in one of the top windows of the house. Lena's father spoke of seeing her often. It is thought that she is one of the two Hansbrough sisters who are buried on the grounds.

Another tale is that of a soldier hiding in the basement of the house during the Civil War. Yankee soldiers were approaching Salubria to pilfer anything of use. The woman of the house took all of the family's silver and hid it in a secret passage. After all that transpired, she was never seen again, and neither was the family silver (Scherquist 2016).

This is a gorgeous property and home. When I visited and spoke with Lena, the wind was really gusting. We heard several noises, but we attributed them to the wind. We could not go to any of the upstairs rooms since there had been some damage to the stairs, and it was unsafe.

SALUBRIA MANOR
19095 SALUBRIA LANE
STEVENSBURG, VA 22741
540-423-1700
TUESDAY–SATURDAY, 1–5PM
HTTP://GERMANNA.ORG/SALUBRIA/

3.

ORANGE

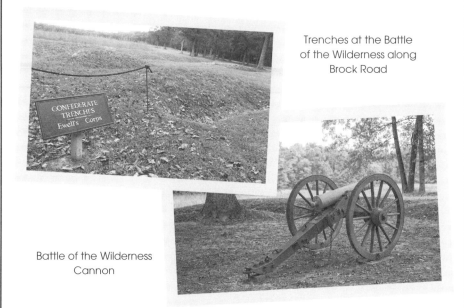

Trenches at the Battle
of the Wilderness along
Brock Road

Battle of the Wilderness
Cannon

BATTLE OF THE WILDERNESS

The surprising thing about this skirmish is where it was fought. This battle took place in an old corn patch, with both sides, the Confederate and Union soldiers, getting into a fistfight along the way. It is called the Wilderness because there are more than seventy miles of trees and forests to traipse to find specific battle sites (Audibert 2011).

Between May 5 and 7, 1864, the opening skirmishes took place between Robert E. Lee and Ulysses S. Grant. The fighting was hectic while both sides tried to move around in the forest of trees and tall grass. Visibility was nonexistent, making it hard to see where the enemy hid. The soldiers were able to regroup when the sun set on the Wilderness. The next day, many generals lost their lives in the epic battle, but Grant refused to give up. He stated he would fight all summer if need be (Civil War Trust 2017a). Grant's plan was to destroy Lee's army. If Lee fell, then so would Richmond. Lee was heavily outnumbered both in troops and guns. Grant had roughly 65,000 more soldiers, and his weapons were far superior to Lee's (Civil War Trust 2017b).

On May 7, the battle moved toward the outskirts of Spotsylvania Courthouse. Close to 163,000 soldiers fought in this battle; over 30,000 lost their lives fighting for their respective sides (Civil War Trust 2017a). The trees in the battlefield still hold cannonballs in their bark, and sometimes, tourists find remnants of the battle that waged long ago. One person reported finding an old, war-ravaged boot with the skeletal foot still inside it. Still lying covered beneath the dirt, many soldiers never made it back home (McKendry 2016b).

Many reports of ghostly activity and the battle still being fought are widespread among visitors. Tidewater Paranormal recorded elevated electromagnetic field (EMF) fluctuations at Higgerson and Chewning Farms. The trenches on Brock Road also had activity (Tidewater Paranormal 2013). Tapp Field pictures presented many orbs (www.tidewaterparanormal.yolasite.com/evidence.php).

Visitors report hearing cannon fire and gunfire along with screams of men fighting for their lives (McKendry 2016b). One visitor took a picture of a long expanse of the battlefield. After she examined each image, she discovered a shadow figure in one of them that could have been a soldier or a hooded person. Some see two figures, and some see nothing at all (Fair 2008).

A ghostly woman is seen in the woods, sometimes calling to her husband, Jacob, who is believed to have been killed in the war. Soldiers have been seen marching down the fields as well as lying in the trenches. People driving near the battle site have reported flashes of light like a cannon or gun being fired (Shadowlands Haunted Places Index 1998).

Hooded figure in Battle of the Wilderness Woods. It can be hard to make out this image, but look closely to see it.

Ghostly face captured in Battle of the Wilderness woods

Does the bloody battle continue to this day where it was first fought? From the evidence presented above, there are ghostly entities still trying to hold on to that piece of land. When my brother and I visited the battlefield, I took my recording device to see if I could pick up any of the above-described sounds. The only place I caught something was at the forest trail at Orange Plank Road. More than 1,200 people perished in these woods, and I felt like someone was watching as we walked the trail. On my recording device, there are several instances of unintelligible speaking by someone; however, it was neither my brother nor I. At two other places, loud growls are heard even though there were no dogs or any other animal around us at the time. I also heard a sound like a cannon firing at one point, but a motorcycle went past right before, so it could have been a backfire. I feel like these woods may hold more secrets than they told me that day, and I definitely want to go back and explore some more.

BATTLE OF THE WILDERNESS
SPOTSYLVANIA AND ORANGE COUNTIES, VIRGINIA
35347 CONSTITUTION HIGHWAY, LOCUST GROVE, VA 22508
540-786-2880
WWW.CIVILWAR.ORG/VISIT/BATTLEFIELDS/WILDERNESS-BATTLEFIELD
RESEARCH BEFORE VISITING; MAPS AND OTHER HELPFUL BROCHURES ARE
AVAILABLE.

ELLWOOD MANOR

Ellwood Manor

William Jones built this Georgian framed home, located within the confines of the Battle of the Wilderness site, in 1781. The house was employed by the V Corps and used as a headquarters for General G. K. Warren during the battle. Grant also met with Warren here to discuss strategy. The manor has hosted many generals, presidents, and foreign dignitaries in its time, including Robert E. Lee and his father, the Marquis de Lafayette, James Madison, James Monroe, and Stonewall Jackson. It is the last remaining structure left from the horrible and bloody battle (Taylor 1991).

Perhaps the most famous object at Ellwood Manor is Stonewall Jackson's left arm. Placed in its own burial site beyond the home on May 2, 1863, visitors can find it nestled right beside a cornfield under a giant oak tree. Jackson suffered an injury by accident from his own troops. A surgeon removed the limb and buried it where it lies today as the only grave marked on the grounds (Eastern National n.d.).

Toward the end of the battle, the house was wrecked almost beyond repair. Looking out the back door, the gardens had been trampled, and many graves littered the property. Inside the manor, the floors were stained with the blood of the people who fought there.

A number of strange occurrences have been witnessed in and around the Manor. Visitors report seeing flashing lights in one of the upstairs bedrooms. Music and singing are heard when no one is in the house; when the noise is investigated, the radio is found to be unplugged. One of the doors to a room upstairs opens and closes by itself. There is also a story about a young lover shooting himself and leaving his blood all over the floor. It supposedly remained there for more than fifty years until it was painted over by new owners.

The burial site of Stonewall Jackson's arm

Ellwood Manor holds an interesting history from both the battle fought there and its unique gravesite in the back. This should definitely be on your list to visit while seeing the Wilderness Battlefield.

ELLWOOD MANOR
120 CHATHAM LANE
FREDERICKSBURG, VA 22405
540-693-3200
WWW.NPS.GOV/FRSP/LEARN/HISTORYCULTURE/ELLWOOD.HTM

THE INN AT WILLOW GROVE
(WILLOW GROVE PLANTATION)

Upon first seeing the Inn at Willow Grove, you get a sense of history, and serene calm settles over you. Sitting at the foothills of the Blue Ridge Mountains and constructed by those who also built Montpelier for James Madison, this manor is steeped in presidential history. Built upon grounds once owned by Zachary Taylor and employing one of Thomas Jefferson's architects, the inn has expanded since being built in 1778 (Haunted Places 2016c). The current inn contains seven bedrooms with private baths and a magnificent kitchen that serves dinner Thursday through Sunday (Fox 1994). Behind the property, there is a stunning view that shouldn't be missed as one is looking over the mountains and city below in the valley.

The Inn at Willow Grove

Battles have taken place on the tract's lush grounds in the past. Both the Revolutionary and Civil Wars brought encampments and headquarter sites to the property, and guests can still find deep trenches all over the grounds (Fox 1994).

A manor immersed in this much history dictates that there are a few ghosts that may have decided to stay at and not check out of the inn. Many guests have mentioned the astral spirits to the owners and staff. One is a younger man who is seen with a young woman in the parlor in the early morning hours. Another is an African American woman with her two children who are walking down the hallways (Fox 1994). A legend connected to the woman states she was a slave who took care of the owner's children in addition to her own two. Apparently, the owner was also the father of her two children. He had all of them killed, and it is said they are buried on the property; however, their graves are unmarked. She is believed to be searching for her dead children (Kinney 2009).

One owner noticed clothes missing after they were laid out at night. This particular room was not finished yet, so the door stayed closed during the night. A few weeks later, the missing clothes appeared; they had been washed and neatly folded (Taylor 2007).

There are many reports of voices and other noises coming from empty rooms, as well as people walking up the hallways. No one is seen when these noises are investigated. Outside, the spirits of two Confederate soldiers have been encountered resting under the large trees in front of the inn.

INN AT WILLOW GROVE
14079 PLANTATION WAY
ORANGE, VA 22960
540-672-5982
WWW.WILLOWGROVEINN.COM

MAYHURST INN

Mayhurst Inn

With luxurious surroundings and gorgeous views, Mayhurst Inn is the ideal location for a getaway or a wedding. The owners take pride in presenting the experience of a lifetime and seal the deal with their southern charm. The magnificent inn has a spiraling staircase that travels up three stories. Many historic figures have traversed these grounds, including A. P. Hill, Robert E. Lee, and Stonewall Jackson (Mayhurst Inn 2017a).

John Willis built the Italian Victorian mansion around 1859 for his wife and their eight children. He was a great-nephew of James Madison and well known among the military. Willis worked as a circuit court judge and founded Orange and Alexandria Railroad (LaLand 2011). He was such an ardent supporter of the Confederacy that he lost most of the property when he couldn't pay taxes in 1868. He was appalled later when a Northern carpetbagger bought the land to invest for the government (Mayhurst Inn 2017b).

The interesting thing to note about the house is that all the windows are from the original structure. The manor stood abandoned for many years and even sustained water damage, but the original building is still standing. Guests are allowed to go metal detecting and have found many remnants from the war, such as belt buckles, jacket buttons, and bullets (LaLand 2011).

Ghostly occurrences have been reported on several travel sites. These incidents concern windows and doors opening by themselves in certain rooms, especially the Madison. Guests also report feelings of being watched when they are staying at the inn. Are there still soldiers watching the property, or is it John Willis watching over his beloved home?

MAYHURST INN
12460 MAYHURST LANE
ORANGE, VA 22960
540-672-5597
WWW.MAYHURSTINN.COM

ZACHARY TAYLOR HOUSE

Zachary Taylor House

Zachary Taylor, the twelfth president of the United States, came from a prominent and wealthy family. He was born on November 24, 1784, at Montebello and was the third child of Colonel Richard and Sarah Taylor. The family sold their former plantation, Hare Forest, and they were looking for a new home to lay down roots (Presidential Avenue 2012). They were quarantined at Montebello because of a measles outbreak and high fever (Taylor 2015). The Taylor family lived in one of the outbuildings from Montebello, probably a log cabin. However, none of the original outbuildings exist today (Presidential Avenue 2012).

Montebello, built in the late 1800s, is situated in the middle of rolling hills with great views of the Blue Ridge Mountains. Today, it has two stories and a whole host of other attributes, including a guest house, pool, barn, and multiple storage facilities (Antique Properties 2009). The historic home is built in the Greek Revival style and complemented with seven anterior columns.

Another historical connection exists between Zachary Taylor and his son-in-law. His daughter Sarah married Jefferson Davis, who became president of the Confederate States of America during the Civil War (Taylor 2015).

Ghostly occurrences abound at the historic mansion. Noises are heard upstairs when no one is present in those rooms. Music that sounds like violins playing is heard quite frequently in the main rooms of the house. Some residents have seen a couple coming down the staircase at different intervals. When they are asked who they are, they simply vanish (Shadowlands Haunted Places Index 1998).

MONTEBELLO
ZACHARY TAYLOR HOUSE
7350 SPOTTSWOOD TRAIL & OLD MONTEBELLO DRIVE
GORDONSVILLE, VA 22942
THERE IS A HISTORICAL MARKER OUT FRONT, BUT THIS IS A PRIVATELY OWNED RESIDENCE.

GORDON-BARBOUR ELEMENTARY SCHOOL

Gordon-Barbour Elementary School

Gordon-Barbour is filled with caring teachers and parents who want their children to succeed from an early age. They have great standards-of-learning (SOL) scores and are very active in the community. Having both academics and sports in its curriculum, the school starts with core classes and branches out into the arts and languages (Virginia Department of Education n.d.).

The ghost story that surrounds the school is a sad one. It seems a child named Mojo left her grandmother's necklace in her locker by accident. They were demolishing part of the school where her locker just happened to be located. She thought she had time to go back and retrieve the item, but they wound up tearing down that section before she made it back outside; the rubble and debris crushed her. Some say they have seen her reflection in the mirror behind them in the girl's bathroom (Ghosts of America n.d.j).

GORDON-BARBOUR ELEMENTARY SCHOOL
500 WEST BAKER STREET
GORDONSVILLE, VA 22942
540-661-4500
HTTPS://SITES.GOOGLE.COM/A/OCSS-VA.ORG/GBES

EXCHANGE HOTEL

Exchange Hotel

The Exchange Hotel is filled with history and charm; it is also the home for many wayward spirits who have not yet found their way home. Built in 1860, the hotel was comparable to a Hilton today. The building was known as the Exchange Hotel since its location by the train tracks and depot allowed soldiers and other travelers to exchange trains in their journey. Trains could also refuel with needed wood and water. Rooms ran around $1.25 a night, and for some folks that was more than they could afford. These people could be found on the front lawn or down by the tracks while they waited for the next train to arrive (DiMaggio 2011).

In 1862, during the Civil War, the hotel became a major hospital, treating more than 70,000 soldiers on both sides of the war. Over 700 were buried on the grounds surrounding the property. After 1865, and the end of the war, the hospital became the Freedman's Bureau Hospital. Freed ex-slaves could come to the facility to get needed medical treatment, a meal, and even a job in some cases (Charlottesville Haunts and History 2011).

Today, the building is known as the Civil War Museum at the Exchange Hotel. They have cataloged many artifacts and found more pieces in hidden spots on the property. One is under the stairs of the main house, where they discovered many relics showing that a soldier had been placed there because all the hospital beds were taken (Sykes 2017). They have also refurbished the hotel to make it look like it did back when it was a tavern and a stopover between trains. There is a hospital room, tavern, train station, and schoolroom to show what life was like back in those days (Exchange Hotel 2015).

The building next door to the hotel was employed as the main kitchen. There is a "whistle walk" from that building to the hotel. Slaves bringing food to people had to whistle on the way over to the hotel. The owner knew that if they were whistling, they couldn't be eating the food (Sykes 2016).

The Exchange Hotel is well known for its ghostly occurrences. They have several entities that cause mischief throughout the hotel and building next door. I enjoyed a four-hour evening tour and ghost hunt in April 2017. We learned about the building and its surrounding property. We also spent some time sitting in specific rooms that were known to have activity to see if we could get the spirits to communicate with us by way of flashlight or voice box.

We started the night tour with a discussion of the history and spooky occurrences in the three buildings: main building, kitchen, and train depot. The train depot was closed for renovations. The main building has three floors, whereas the kitchen building has two. All the rooms hold period pieces to give the visitor an idea of what the hotel may have looked like back in the Civil War.

The first room you step into is the gift shop, which is just inside the back door of the main building. There is a postcard holder on one of the tables near the door that has been filmed turning by itself. The video is at www.hgiexchange.com/exchange-hotel/evidence-collection (Sykes 2017).

Ghostly activity is at an all-time high when trains are running past the hotel in the evening. The spirits who still inhabit the rooms think there are more soldiers and people coming to the hotel to visit. Several trains came down the rail while we were on the tour, and the atmosphere seemed electric in nature, like there was excitement. The most electronic voice phenomena (EVPs) they have gotten at the hotel is eighty in five minutes (Sykes 2017).

Our tour guide this particular night was Missy Sykes. She was well versed in the history and the entities that still roam the old hotel. As soon as I walked in the door, I could feel pushes and pulls in all directions. I could tell this place had not only a history, but a few spirits hanging around as well. I felt most were gentle and kind; however, as I learned on the tour, some were not always like this—they could be quite mischievous (Sykes 2017).

One of the interesting things they had displayed was a poster board with many pictures and images seen within those pictures. They had orbs, lights, and other people in the pictures who weren't there when they were taken. They also have one portrait on the second floor of a woman who will slowly change into a man if you look long enough.

Missy told us of a volunteer who was outside walking around in front of the museum one night. He happened to take a picture of one of the third-floor windows. The pictures show a little girl, who they think is Emma, since she stays along the third-floor hallway. No one else was in the hotel at the time (Sykes 2017).

Two college girls took a photo of the mirror on the second floor. Between them, you can spot a doctor or nurse who wasn't present when the picture was taken. In a similar vein, another tourist took pictures of some of the second-floor windows from the inside. He found someone standing beside him in one of the photos, and he was alone at the time (Sykes 2017).

Two pictures from the train depot showed, in one, a clear image, and, in the other, a shadow man. There were three people in the depot at the time, but one picture clearly shows a fourth person. They have no clue who he is (Sykes 2017).

Many ghostly characters roam the halls to this day; read what follows about each room that has activity and what the occurrences are. Each room has its own story and furnishings to show the look of the hotel during the Civil War era.

First Floor, Train Room: The Gordonsville sign is an original piece from the Train Depot during the Civil War. The ticket windows are the actual ones from the depot first built on the property. There is not a lot of activity in this room, but you can see shadows moving under the door some nights (Sykes 2017).

First Floor, Tavern Room: Across from the Train Room, this space has been converted into a study. It is an active room, and women have to be wary when they go to the bathroom down the hall. The door gets stuck at times. A tall, dark figure stands in the hallway, and he likes to hold the door shut as a joke. If you ask him nicely to release the door, it will open easily (Sykes 2017). I have had this happen to me twice.

Second Floor, Ella's Room: In this active room there is a picture of a pretty woman that is hanging above the fireplace. This picture was purchased at an auction and hung on the wall at the hotel. It is not original to the property. When some EVPs were performed, they heard someone ask, "Who found Ella?" They don't really know if that is the lady's name; however, it seemed to fit, so they named her Ella. People on the ghost tour who stand before the picture, with just a flashlight on, will see her face slowly turn into a man. Pictures taken of the portrait show a frown, but they will turn into a smile if you watch (Sykes 2017).

Second Floor, George Bagby's Room: The old bathtub also came from an auction and was placed in this active room to give a look of the period. George Bagby was a practicing physician brought to the Exchange Hotel. Any females who come into this room should bring a male friend with them, since the doctor can be very frisky. A psychic visited and said he saw a woman on the bed being attacked by a man (Sykes 2017).

Second Floor, Parlor Room: There is a gorgeous chocolate-serving set by the front window. Women often hung out in this room drinking tea and socializing. Missy took three pictures in front of the mirror, and two came out fine. When she looked at the third one, there was a skeletal figure right beside her. The piano is known to play by itself at times (Sykes 2017).

Second Floor, Surgical Room: This is one of my favorite rooms, due to my nursing background, and many strange occurrences have happened in here as well. There is an original Civil War surgical table in the center of the room with bloodstains underneath if you care to look. There is also an original ambulance wagon purchased from an antique dealer. Don't play with the ether mask on the table, though; it was one used back in the Civil War days (Sykes 2017).

They had to break the wagon down into three pieces to get it up the stairs and into the Surgical Room. While they were trying to place the wheels back on, Missy asked the other person in the room to come help them. Angel, a coworker, asked who she was talking to at the time. Missy said she was talking to the man standing over by the door. She got up and looked again, but there was nobody else in the room. They both figured it was one of their husbands playing a joke, and Missy ran downstairs to catch them. She found both of them on the front lawn, working on a separate project and not having any idea what she was talking about with them being upstairs. Missy told Angel what they said and then headed back upstairs. When she got to the top of the stairs, she saw the man standing in the doorway again. She asked him if he was real, and he vanished. Luckily, Angel had witnessed the whole thing (Sykes 2017).

Missy and her family were participating in a reenactment one day and were showing the ways that surgeons used instruments in the Civil War. Her brother was playing a surgeon, and her son portrayed a patient having his arm amputated. Her son had on two long-sleeve shirts at the time. When her brother began to use a sawing motion over her son's arm, he screamed out in pain. Her brother swore the saw never touched her son. When they pulled up his sleeve, he had a deep cut on his arm in the same place the saw would have been. They all thought the ghosts figured they were making fun of them, and this was their way of saying "stop it" (Sykes 2017).

Third Floor, Civil War Equipment Room: This room is full of antiquities, guns, coins, and different ammunition. There is a speaker in one corner of the room that plays music, and it turns on and off by itself. There is a fourteen-year-old boy named Todd that inhabits this room. They are not sure who he is or where he is from, but when he wants to play, he will tap on the glass case in the room (Sykes 2017).

Third Floor, Safety Room: In the middle of the hallway, both Missy and Angel use this room for protection and to recharge. Two nuns stayed here during the war, since there were no nurses. They came from Georgia to care for the sick and wounded. There is no activity in this room at all, and they think it is *because* it was the nun's room (Sykes 2017).

Third Floor, Secret Service Room: Brand-new room being furnished at present. No activity noted in here as of yet (Sykes 2017).

Third Floor, School Room: Missy refuses to enter this room, since she has been attacked by the spirit who inhabits it. There is a man named Bill, a horrible drunk, and he hides in the back closet. The first time Missy was attacked, she was standing by the closet door, telling a group about the paranormal, and something brushed against her. She started to feel so bad that it was hard to breathe; she assumed Bill was telling her to leave his premises (Sykes 2017).

There is no door on the room because they like it to be quiet while they are doing the ghost tours and investigations. On several nights during tours, the door on the room would continually slam shut, interrupting everyone's investigations. They took the door off, thinking they'd solved the problem. However, the slamming still occurs because Bill now slams the closet door to cause a ruckus (Sykes 2017).

They have also found out that Bill intimidates Emma, the little girl who stays in the hallway. She usually starts to quiet down around ten or eleven at night because Bill has told her it is past her bedtime (Sykes 2017).

Third Floor, Barracks Room: Two ladies were taking a tour one night and had stayed upstairs awfully late. One of the staff went up to tell them it was time to leave for the night, and they apologized for keeping them there. They were having such an interesting conversation with the one-legged soldier in the room. The staff person asked, "What soldier with one leg?" The ladies had thought he was a reenactor, so they chatted with him about the times he was portraying. One visitor took a photo of the room and found the apparition of a one-legged soldier sitting on a bed. He does hide under a specific bed in the room and will grab your leg at times when you walk past (Sykes 2017).

Third Floor, Hallway: Emma, the little girl between nine and twelve, hangs out in this part of the hotel. She loves people to sing to her, especially "Ring around the Rosie" or "London Bridge." When they researched to find out more about Emma, all they found was that a little girl named Emma lived on the property, but no death record was available (Sykes 2017).

Many children died at the hotel because of its location next to the train tracks. The original owner, Richard Omohundro, walked over to his stables one day, located where the BBQ Exchange is currently. Unbeknown to him, his son, between the age of one and three, followed him, was hit by a train, and died. The hotel has some pictures of the boy, and when they ask his name during investigations, he only giggles (Sykes 2017).

They also know of the children because they saw tracks in the water after mopping the back hallway. They seemed to be the size of a nine-year-old child. Whether it is Emma or the little boy who was killed on the tracks, they do not know (DiMaggio 2011).

First Floor, Second Building: We moved onto the smaller kitchen building next door. There are no lights in the kitchen, but there are some upstairs. A cook named Anna, who is described as four feet tall and mean as a snake, haunts the kitchen. When asked at an investigation what she was cooking, the response was "I cook fried chicken" (DiMaggio 2011). Many people hear such things as doors slamming or something being moved across the floor. It is extremely active here, since there is also a young boy, around fourteen or fifteen, who haunts this area. The staff calls him Cornbread (Sykes 2017).

Back in Civil War days, if an African American man was caught looking at a white woman, that was an automatic reason for the soldiers to kill him. Cornbread had glanced at a white woman walking past him, and the soldiers saw him. They chased him to the kitchen, where he tried to hide to no avail. The soldiers hanged him in the stairwell of the building. He is a very playful entity (Sykes 2017).

Second Floor, Second Building, Olivia's Room: I had some very strong feelings in this room, and the air was a little heavier as well. Olivia worked at brothels on Main Street during the Civil War. She got pushed out of one of the brothels, so she stayed at the hotel. She would still sell herself to the soldiers as they came through on the train. She is very active whenever the trains go past, and she loves the menfolk (Sykes 2017).

One tourist threw out a dollar on the floor, but he received no response. Missy explained this was an insult to Olivia, who worked hard for her money. He threw out $100 and immediately felt a pressure on his lap. When he reached over to pick up the $100, the pressure immediately dissipated (Sykes 2017).

Second Floor, Second Building, Major Richard's Room: The entity in this room can be very mean, and he will push people down the stairway. Ensure that you hold the rail while ascending or descending the steps. He is also very active when a train goes past the hotel. He used to be the greeter for soldiers and other people getting off the trains. After much research, they found he murdered his wife in this room. He thought she was having an affair, so he slashed her throat open (Sykes 2017).

Train Depot: This building housed the platform where people would wait to exchange trains to head to Richmond or Charlottesville. The depot was constructed in 1841 and may have been one of Orange's first stations. Between June 1863 and May 1864, over 23,000 soldiers on both sides of the war were brought here for medical treatment (James 2016). The sad part is that the hotel alone could not hold

Train Depot and Hanging Tree

all the soldiers at times. They placed the dead in the depot until they could be buried. Some of the living were also placed in the depot for lack of room. They died out of fright or from just being around the corpses (Sykes 2017).

There are ghost trains that travel down these tracks as well. Missy told stories of some nights when they will hear a whistle blow and the arms go down across the track. They will go outside and wait fifteen to twenty minutes, with no train in sight. The arms rise like a train has gone past (Sykes 2017).

There is also a story about homeless people living down near the tracks. The hotel was empty at the time, and they were asked why they didn't just stay inside for shelter on cold nights. They replied that at night, shadows could be seen walking across the front porch and first floor of the hotel. None of them wanted any part of that (Sykes 2017).

GHOSTLY INVESTIGATION

We headed to the third floor of the main building and hoped to make contact with Emma. Missy turned out all the lights as we used the voice box and the REM Pod (antennae and different-colored lights go off when there is motion near the pod). Most of us sat on the bench near the schoolroom, with others in the hallway. We set the REM Pod in a backroom, where no one could set it off accidentally. All through the EVP session, the REM Pod would continually light up in alarm.

At one point, there was an unusual tapping noise that sounded like it was coming from someone sitting on the bench. I looked down to see if someone was just nervously drumming their fingers, but everyone had their hands in front of them, holding a piece of equipment or just waiting to see what would happen next.

As Missy started the voice box, she began asking questions. She also explained that Emma loved several songs, and if someone would sing them, she might be more participative. So one of our group started singing "Ring around the Rosie," and another sang "London Bridge."

MISSY ASKED, "CAN YOU TURN ON THE FLASHLIGHT FOR ME?"
IT TOOK A FEW MOMENTS, BUT THE FLASHLIGHT SHINED BRIGHTLY.
"CAN YOU TELL US YOUR NAME?"
RESPONSE: "IN A SECOND."
"HOW MANY OF YOU ARE HERE?"
RESPONSE: "8." I TOOK THIS TO MEAN THE EIGHT SPIRITS MISSY HAD ALREADY TOLD US ABOUT IN THE MAIN BUILDING.
"IS EMMA HERE WITH US?"
RESPONSE: WE HEARD A LITTLE GIRL MAKING COOING-TYPE SOUNDS, BUT NO WORDS WERE HEARD.
THE REM POD WAS GOING OFF EVERY FEW SECONDS AT THIS POINT.
"TELL ME HOW MANY PEOPLE ARE HERE."
RESPONSE: "WE ARE ALL STILL HERE."

After about forty-five minutes, we headed to George Bagby's room to investigate and see if we could get him to talk with us as well. The REM Pod continually went off in here as well. We placed it near the bathtub while the group stayed on the other side of the room.

"CAN YOU TOUCH THE REM POD AND MAKE IT LIGHT UP?"
RESPONSE: THE GREEN LIGHT ON THE REM POD WOULD LIGHT UP EVERY TIME. IT WAS THE ONLY COLOR USED.
AFTER SOME QUIET, MISSY ASKED IF HE WAS STILL IN THE ROOM.
RESPONSE: GREEN LIGHT LIT UP.
"CAN YOU TOUCH THE RED LIGHT THIS TIME?"
RESPONSE: THE RED LIGHT LIT UP.
"IF YOU LIKE US BEING HERE, TOUCH IT AGAIN."
RESPONSE: NO RESPONSE; I TOOK THAT TO MEAN HE DIDN'T LIKE US BEING IN HIS ROOM.
THE FLASHLIGHT MISSY HAD PLACED ON THE FIREPLACE MANTEL STARTED TO SHINE SOFTLY AT FIRST AND THEN GO VERY BRIGHT, THEN IT DIMMED OUT SLOWLY. HE STARTED LIGHTING UP THE REM POD AGAIN, BUT THIS TIME, BOTH THE RED AND GREEN LIGHTS WERE LIT.
"ARE YOU TAKING A BATH?"
RESPONSE: NO RESPONSE.
"WHERE DID YOU GO?"
RESPONSE: REM POD LIGHTS UP AGAIN.

We stayed in Bagby's room around forty minutes before heading to the second building's kitchen. There were chairs lined up against the inside wall, so we all settled down to see what would happen here. It was completely dark in the kitchen except for the lights on the REM Pod. Missy started to ask questions to see whom we might communicate with here.

"ANYONE HERE? CAN YOU COME TALK TO US?"
RESPONSE: NO RESPONSE.
"CORNBREAD, ARE YOU HERE?"
RESPONSE: NO RESPONSE.
"CAN YOU TOUCH ONE OF THE DEVICES AND LIGHT IT UP FOR US?"
RESPONSE: NO RESPONSE.
"HOW ABOUT OLIVIA? ARE YOU HERE? CAN YOU MAKE A NOISE?"
RESPONSE: NO RESPONSE.
"CAN YOU TURN ON THE FLASHLIGHT FOR US?"
RESPONSE: FLASHLIGHT TURNED ON.
"CAN YOU TURN IT BACK OFF? IS THIS CORNBREAD? CAN YOU TURN THE LIGHT BACK OFF?"
RESPONSE: LIGHT TURNED OFF.
"IS ANNA THE COOK HERE?"
RESPONSE: NO RESPONSE.
"CORNBREAD, ARE YOU AFRAID OF THE SOLDIERS?"
RESPONSE: NO RESPONSE.

At this point, Missy stated she saw shadows moving across the top of the stairs. She thought maybe it was Cornbread, and she asked him to come down and join us.

RESPONSE: FLASHLIGHT CAME ON.
"CAN YOU TURN IT BACK OFF FOR ME?"
RESPONSE: FLASHLIGHT TURNED COMPLETELY OFF.
SHE ASKED IF SHE SAID THEIR NAME, THEY SHOULD TURN THE LIGHT BACK ON.
"IS IT CORNBREAD?"
RESPONSE: NO RESPONSE.
"IS IT OLIVIA?"
RESPONSE: NO RESPONSE.
"IS IT MAJOR RICHARDS?"
 RESPONSE: NO RESPONSE.
"IS IT BEA?"
RESPONSE: NO RESPONSE.
"IS IT SARAH?"
 RESPONSE: NO RESPONSE.
"ARE YOU THE ONE WHO SLAMMED THE DOOR ON US LAST WEEK UPSTAIRS?"

RESPONSE: NO RESPONSE.
"DO YOU WANT US TO COME UPSTAIRS AND TALK WITH YOU?"
RESPONSE: NO RESPONSE.

At this point, we weren't getting too much, so Missy suggested we move to the upstairs rooms to investigate. One of the people on the tour had gotten cold feet, so Missy asked Cornbread to reassure him that everything would be fine.

"CORNBREAD, CAN YOU TURN THE LIGHT ON AND TELL HIM HE WILL BE JUST FINE?"
"DID YOU HEAR THAT? IT SOUNDED LIKE SOMEONE JUST SAID 'YEAH'!" (MISSY)

I did hear something on the recording, but I could not discern what it was after many playbacks.

The light finally came back on to verify that all would be fine, and Cornbread would watch out for us as we journeyed upstairs.

"ALL RIGHT, CORNBREAD, WE ARE GOING UPSTAIRS; WILL YOU COME WITH US? IF YOU ARE HERE, PLEASE TURN THE LIGHT OFF."
RESPONSE: THERE WAS A FLICKER IN THE LIGHT.
ONE OF THE TOUR MEMBERS ASKED IF CORNBREAD WOULD TURN THE LIGHT OFF FOR HIM.
RESPONSE: LIGHT TURNED OFF.

Missy stated she was seeing more shadows upstairs as time passed. We decided to make our way up to the second floor and started in Olivia's room. As soon as I stepped in the room, I noticed it was very heavy and hot. This was much different from the first time we had visited, when it was freezing cold. Remembering that it was March weather outside, I wondered what brought on the temperature change in such a short amount of time.

Missy explained that many EVPs had been captured in the room. Most were of a female moaning. Since Olivia had been a prostitute, this may have been an explanation for that sound.

"OLIVIA, ARE YOU HERE?"
RESPONSE: NO RESPONSE.
"DO YOU HAVE A CLIENT AT PRESENT? CAN YOU TOUCH THE REM POD ON THE FLOOR?"
RESPONSE: REM POD LIT UP.
"DO YOU LIKE THE PRETTY DRESS WE HAVE FOR YOU?"
RESPONSE: REM POD WENT OFF AGAIN.

"DO YOU LIKE ALL THE PEOPLE I BROUGHT TO VISIT YOU? TOUCH THE REM POD
IF YOU DO."
RESPONSE: REM POD LIT UP GREEN.
"IS MAJOR RICHARDS HERE?"
RESPONSE: NO RESPONSE.

We didn't get a lot of response from the upstairs portion of the second building, so we headed down to the Train Depot to learn about the Hanging Tree—a tall, foreboding tree that stands in front of the depot. Taller slaves were hanged from the higher branches. On clear nights, you may get apparitions in your pictures near the branches. The Train Depot was closed, so we could not investigate there.

We returned to the third-floor hallway to investigate again. As soon as we got there and settled into our seats, the REM Pod started going off again.

"EMMA, IS THAT YOU?"
RESPONSE: REM POD CONTINUALLY GOES OFF.
MISSY EXPLAINED SHE LOVED TO PLAY WITH THE REM POD BECAUSE OF THE
PRETTY COLORS.
"WERE YOU AFRAID OF SOME OF THE OTHER PEOPLE WHO WERE HERE?"
RESPONSE: REM POD LIT UP AGAIN FOR A QUICK BEAT AS IF SHE WAS SAYING
YES.
AUTHOR'S NOTE: THERE WERE A FEW PEOPLE ON OUR TOUR WHO PROBABLY
SHOULD NOT HAVE BEEN THERE.
"ARE YOU GLAD WE CAME BACK TO SEE YOU?"
RESPONSE: ONE BEAT LIGHT—YES.
"DO YOU WANT US TO SING TO YOU?"
RESPONSE: LITTLE GIRL SOUNDS ARE MADE, AND THE REM POD GOES OFF.
"DO YOU GUYS [TOUR GROUP] WANT ME TO GO GET THE OVILUS?" (THE OVILUS
IS ANOTHER TYPE OF VOICE BOX FOR COMMUNICATION.)

We all agreed it would be something different, and wanted to see how it would differ from the voice box. The REM Pod also lit up again, so we figured Emma liked the idea as well. Missy left to go downstairs. The REM Pod started to light up for a very long time, and we asked Emma if she was having fun.

RESPONSE: THE REM POD LIT UP FOR A QUICK BEAT—YES.
"WHICH OF THE FOUR LIGHTS IS YOUR FAVORITE COLOR?"
RESPONSE: ALL LIGHTS LIT UP, BUT GREEN STAYED ON THE LONGEST.

Missy sets up the Ovilus and has it run through all the words. While she is doing this, the REM Pod continually flashes and beeps.

"OKAY, EMMA, I HAVE THE VOICE BOX, SO YOU CAN TALK TO US? CAN YOU COME BACK OVER HERE?"
ANOTHER MEMBER OF THE GROUP ASKED EMMA HOW OLD SHE WAS.
RESPONSE: THERE WERE SOME CHIRPY METALLIC SOUNDS.
THERE WAS QUIET FOR A FEW MINUTES. MISSY ASKED IF BILL HAD CHASED EMMA OFF.
RESPONSE: NO RESPONSE.
"CAN'T YOU COME BACK AND TALK TO US, EMMA? IF ANYONE IS HERE, PLEASE TOUCH THE REM POD. BILL, IF YOU ARE TRYING TO SCARE EMMA, PLEASE LEAVE HER ALONE."
RESPONSE: THE OVILUS DISPLAYED THE WORD HATE.
MISSY EXPLAINED THAT BILL DOES NOT LIKE HER AND HAS ATTACKED HER ON MULTIPLE OCCASIONS.
"WE WANT TO TALK WITH EMMA. PLEASE COME BACK AND LIGHT UP THE REM POD LIKE A RAINBOW. IT IS OKAY."
RESPONSE: REM POD BEGINS TO LIGHT UP AGAIN.
"EMMA, WAS BILL SCARING YOU?"
REM POD GOES OFF AGAIN.
"YOU DON'T HAVE TO BE AFRAID OF HIM; WE CAME TO SEE YOU."
REM POD CONTINUALLY LIGHTS UP ALL OVER.

It becomes quiet again for a while, with Missy and other members of the group asking questions to which there are no responses.

"EMMA, ARE YOU STILL HERE? PLEASE COME BACK AND TALK WITH US."
RESPONSE: THERE ARE SOME NOISES LIKE FOOTSTEPS IN THE BACK HALLWAY, AND THE REM POD KEEPS LIGHTING UP.
"IS BILL TELLING YOU NOT TO TALK TO US?"
RESPONSE: REM POD GOES OFF.
IT BECAME QUIET AGAIN. AFTER A FEW QUESTIONS FOR EMMA THAT WERE NOT ANSWERED, MISSY TRIED ANOTHER SPIRIT.
"IS THE ONE-LEGGED SOLDIER HERE?"
RESPONSE: REM POD GOES OFF.
"EMMA, ARE YOU STILL HERE? BILL, LEAVE EMMA ALONE SO SHE CAN TALK TO US FOR A LITTLE WHILE."
RESPONSE: NO RESPONSE.

Since we had heard from the one-legged soldier, we decided to go to his room and see if we could talk with him. There were no responses to any questions asked. While we were standing in the room, a train went by the hotel. The temperature in the room dropped from warm to very cold.

We decided to end our night in George Bagby's room, which was also very cold. Warm when we did the first visit, Bagby's room seemed to have dropped a few degrees in the interim. There were no responses to questions asked, and we ended our investigation there. We all headed back downstairs to chat about what we had seen and heard. It was a very interesting night that I immensely enjoyed.

EXCHANGE HOTEL
CIVIL WAR MEDICAL MUSEUM
400 SOUTH MAIN STREET
GORDONSVILLE, VA 22942
540-832-2944
WWW.HGIEXCHANGE.COM/
TOURS OF THE MUSEUM ARE IN THE DAYTIME; IT IS CLOSED ON FRIDAYS AND MAJOR HOLIDAYS. NIGHT TOURS CAN BE SCHEDULED ONLINE AT THE WEBSITE OR BY CALLING THE EXCHANGE HOTEL, AND THEY ARE USUALLY HELD ON FRIDAY NIGHTS FROM 8:00 P.M. TO 12 MIDNIGHT.

4.
LOUISA/FLUVANNA
LOUISA

Hall's Store / Green Springs Depot

HALL'S STORE / GREEN SPRINGS DEPOT

Back in the old days, it was believed that the store and the depot had a curse on them. People were wary of getting too close to either location, since there was a history of at least three murders and many fires. The railroad that ran beside them was on the line from Charlottesville to Richmond, transporting produce and supplies to Louisa (Hines 2016).

John Boston started with a broom factory and a small store. When he died, his son, Channing, stepped in to lease these places to profitable businesses. Roy McKnighton was one of the first to lease the property. His lease was revoked after it was found that his brother was killed in a drunken altercation one night while at the store (Hines 2016).

In the next few years, the property came into the ownership of two brothers, Silas and Lewis Yancey. Silas went to Richmond to purchase some goods for the store, and he almost suffocated because of a gas leak. He was taken to emergency care, but there was nothing that could be done. Lewis came to stay with Silas until he died; however, it was later discovered that Silas had been next to a smallpox victim. Lewis, in turn, contracted smallpox, which led to the store being quarantined. Railroad travel stopped temporarily to get the sickness under control. The store became a hospital, and the depot became a detention station for those with smallpox. Lewis survived the outbreak, but Louisa County gave him nothing in return for the use of his businesses. People who were sick also wound up eating all of his food and using his supplies that were originally purchased for his store. He left Louisa broke (Hines 2016).

Over time, others came to purchase the properties. William Richard Dunkum and David Asa Dunkum bought the business in 1905. While they were trying to get the store up and running, they both lost their infant babies to smallpox. Two other men, Isaac Poindexter and T. W. Ross, got into a quarrel, so the local deputies took control of the situation. However, as Poindexter's son was hitching the horses to take his father home, one of the deputies shot him in front of Hall's Store.

David Dunkum died in 1911 from pneumonia. His wife, Lizzie, later married Victor Hall, the town's magistrate, to provide a home for her two daughters. The issue was that she was thirty-eight, while Victor was only twenty-four. Having such an unorthodox arrangement in those days led to heavy criticism at work and in church (Hines 2016).

In early 1913, a huge fire burned down the store and many houses within the town. William Dunkum's store also burned down in April 1914, ironically in the middle of a very heavy rainstorm. Since this was Dunkum's second fire within a year, the insurance company accused him of burning down his own business for the money.

Lizzie begged her husband, Victor, to ensure that no embers from the fires were in danger of burning down their home as well. He went out to check the scene of the fires, and Lizzie later heard him screaming after a gunshot was heard. When Lizzie found Victor, he was in a heap on the floor from a head wound. He was moved to his own bed and passed away around ten that night. While everyone was trying to figure out who harmed Victor, Lizzie tried to make arrangements to get Hall's Store back. She had many things coming in by Green Springs Depot, and she retrieved them with the help of her father-in-law. It was serendipitous, since the arsonist decided to burn down the depot that very night (Hines 2016).

Hall's Store was constantly watched after that, and Lizzie and her daughters discovered another fire in their pantry that night as well. Lizzie was accused of starting both these fires in the pantry and the store. After all, she had just removed her items from the depot before it started burning. They also began wondering if Lizzie hadn't killed Victor just so she could marry another man. There was talk of other murders, such as the McCue murder in Albemarle. She was arrested for the murder, but they released her on bail provided that she stay out of Louisa County. The business would fail, and Lizzie was in quite an amount of debt from the legal bills. She sold the property, store, and contents for $250 and moved to Richmond to await her murder trial.

All the evidence was entirely circumstantial. Victor's gun was still fully loaded—and never fired—so they had no murder weapon. After all this, Lizzie received ten years in jail, where the citizens of Louisa pleaded to the governor to release her. Two years later, the governor pardoned her. She died in 1946 and was buried in Richmond. The arsonist and shooter were never found (Hines 2016).

There are stories of screaming and doors opening when no one is near them. There is a graveyard nearby with victims from smallpox. I ran into someone at another location who said they sometimes see people crossing the railroad tracks beside the store, then suddenly vanish. Perhaps Lizzie has come back to try to clear her name once more.

HALL'S STORE / GREEN SPRINGS DEPOT
DUNKUM STORE ROAD
LOUISA, VA 23093
540-693-3200 EXTENSION 1020 (GREEN SPRINGS PARK AND PLANTATION)
THIS IS A GENERAL ADDRESS; THERE ARE NO STREET ADDRESSES FOR THIS
PARTICULAR LOCATION.

TREVILIAN STATION AND BATTLEFIELD

If you are planning a visit to the battlefield and surrounding areas, go to the website of the Trevilian Station to find a wonderful map and driving tour. It is a very historic site to visit and think about what happened at each location. There are historical markers at each site to tell you what part of the battle happened where, and who was involved. As you drive to the many locations, you can almost imagine the stomping feet, cannons firing, and men screaming from being hit after a fatal gunshot. There are eleven stops on the tour, starting at the Sargent Museum, which also houses the Louisa County Historical Society, where you can peruse maps and other historical information concerning the battle sites. The next stops cover the Louisa Courthouse, where first contact was made; Sheridan's Camp at Clayton's Store, where the first shots were at Bibb's Crossroads; Poindexter House; Netherland Tavern; Custer's First Stand; Ogg Farm Bloody Angle; Oakland Cemetery; and the Exchange Hotel (Trevilian Station n.d.b).

During June 11–12, 1864, the Battle of Trevilian Station was fought in Louisa, Virginia. It was a bloody and mass casualty clash between Ulysses Grant and Robert E. Lee. Under the auspices of the Union Cavalry, Major General Philip Sheridan fought many skirmishes against the Confederate commanders, Major Generals Wade Hampton and Fitzhugh Lee. Unfortunately, Hampton's troops defeated Sheridan by destroying the railroad at Trevilian Station and the bridge at the Rivanna River. Brigadier General George Custer came up from the rear and captured the men in Hampton's troops, but Custer soon became flanked by other soldiers (Trevilian Station n.d.a).

On June 12, Sheridan decided to withdraw and rejoin Grant's army as they traveled down from Charlottesville. Sheridan did not succeed in his goal to destroy the Virginia Central Railroad. The whole debacle did allow time for Grant and his troops to cross the James River unscathed (Trevilian Station n.d.a).

The tour starts with the **Louisa Courthouse**. The Virginia Central Railroad ran through the area back in the days of the Civil War. When Sheridan headed west to get to the railroad first and demolish it, Lee sent General Hampton to protect Confederate areas with more than 6,000 men. Hampton reached the Louisa Courthouse before Sheridan and camped out at the location to impede Sheridan's army from moving forward (Trevilian Station n.d.b).

Louisa Courthouse

The next location is known as **"First Contact."** General Hampton's troops arrived here on June 10, 1864. They surrounded the Virginia Central Railroad and completely blocked General Sheridan's path to get to Gordonsville. At 3:00 a.m. the next day, some of the troops headed up Route 669 to Clayton's Store.

The first shots of the battle were fired here. The skirmish went on for more than half an hour and was considered a substantial battle. General Custer, hearing of the battle, rallied his troops and headed toward Nunn's Creek Road (Trevilian Station n.d.b).

Clayton's Store is marked by a house just north of the intersection. This site served as General Sheridan's headquarters. There were other troops stationed nearby as well, such as those of General Hampton, General Merritt, General Custer, and Colonel Devin. While Sheridan traveled toward Trevilian Station, Custer's army took Nunn's Creek Road on their way to meet up with Sheridan's men (Trevilian Station n.d.b).

The next location is **Bibb's Crossroads**. More than 9,000 men served under General Sheridan. Their one goal was to demolish the Virginia Central Railroad. There were other troops that arrived at the crossroads that day along with Sheridan's troops. Those of Merritt, Devin, and Butler met at Bibb's, where the first shots of the main battle were fired. Another engagement also occurred along Fredericksburg Stage Road (Trevilian Station n.d.b).

This next stop is where Hart's Battery and Hampton's Charge took place. If you look across the street and near the woods to the left, you will see the **Poindexter House**. Colonel William Sackett led his troops of the 9th New York Cavalry in a

Animal image in picture at Ebenezer Church at Bibb's Crossroads. Look closely, because the animal may be difficult to visualize.

battle here, where he was mortally wounded and then buried in the Poindexter yard. Hampton rallied the 6th South Carolina Cavalry against James Hart. They both shot at each other until their guns were empty, and then they sat down with their men to figure out their next move.

As you continue one more mile south on Oakland Road, the **Netherland Tavern** is ahead on the left. The original building that served as the tavern dates back to 1790, but it was torn down in 1950. Hampton commandeered the tavern as his headquarters and slept in their front yard on a bench. The next morning, Hampton and two other officers, Thomas Rosser and Matthew Butler, decided on their strategy for the coming day. The united troops attacked Sheridan's troops near Clayton's Store. This skirmish pushed Sheridan back to the North Anna River (Trevilian Station n.d.b). As I walked through the grounds, I felt like I was being watched the whole time.

On June 11, 1864, Custer's troops marched down Gordonsville Road with Colonel Russell Algers. As they headed west, they spied General Hampton's troops and captured the majority of them. Custer himself wound up carrying the flag for the men, since the guidon bearer was wounded and could not go any farther. Unfortunately, Lee's men arrived to capture Custer and release Hampton's men and horses. Custer's attack on Hampton became a quick disaster, and a commander from Sheridan's forces called for backup when they discovered the issue. Three brigades released a full-force assault and rescued Custer's men. The federal armies would now gain control of the land, the Netherland Tavern, and the railroad that was laid in the area.

Entrance to Netherland Tavern

Around 4:00 p.m. that day, the Confederates attacked but failed in their skirmish. Hampton withdrew and Lee went east. Hampton's troops blocked Sheridan's only route to Gordonsville. June 12 brought the destruction of parts of the Virginia Central Railroad and Trevilian Station. Sheridan withdrew from the fight and made his way to the other side of the North Anna River to stay for the night and regroup. Hampton still held the battlefield tight and tried to keep the railroad protected (Trevilian Station n.d.b).

There are over sixty men from the Confederate side buried at **Oakland Cemetery**. The sad part is that many of them were never identified. Inside the front gates are the graves of the three Towles brothers: Robert, J. Vivian, and James. Robert was killed near Louisa Courthouse, and his two brothers were disinterred and brought here to rest with him by their father, John. The 7th Georgia Cavalry had over a thirty percent loss in their men the first day they fought. The cemetery is right next to the railroad today. When my brother and I were there visiting, a huge black locomotive went barreling down the track.

Many cemeteries have hauntings. People have seen a soldier running across the road near the cemetery and vanishing afterward. The gates also act funny at times, opening and closing by themselves and sometimes being very hard to open. I noticed this when my brother and I visited the site. When I was there alone another day, they opened right up. I saw no rust or faulty hinges. Could it be a stubborn guard who refuses to let people visit at certain times? There are three interesting graves in the Oakland Cemetery. Two are parents, and the third one is their child. The thing to notice is that the parents' headstones are facing the child's stone. I thought maybe they wanted to be able to see their child for eternity as they are buried on either side of the child.

Train running beside
Oakland Cemetery

Parents' stones facing
different way than child

Trevilian Station was considered one of the huge cavalry battles in the Civil War that employed many troops from either side. Lee's army depended on the location for their supplies during the war. Many men were lost during these battles. Over 9,000 men were killed, wounded, or declared missing from Sheridan's Union troops. On the Confederate side, over 6,000 were lost. After this historic battle and confrontation between the two sides, many of the wounded were taken for medical care to the Exchange Hotel in Gordonsville, which had been turned into a Civil War hospital (Trevilian Station n.d.b).

What is interesting to note is that more than 15,000 soldiers took part in the epic battle. Many people who visit the previously mentioned locations see and hear things that show that there are soldiers still fighting to hold on to a specific location for their leaders. One person lives in a house that is located in a big field in the Trevilian Battlefield. They have caught many images of figures walking through the house, as well as many voice recordings. By far the most scary thing is that one night as they were walking through their house, something grabbed them at the ankle as they walked past. They also heard a stampede going through the home in the middle of the night, and the next morning, they found the carpet covered in hoof prints (Ghosts of America n.d.f).

I spoke to some people who live in the area. They are always hearing the fire of cannons, screaming and yelling, and what sounds like people running through their house. When they get up to look outside, nothing is ever there. They live within walking distance to a couple of haunted spots in the battlefield. They stated it is an ongoing thing, and they have tried to get some paranormal researchers to come and investigate the area.

TREVILIAN STATION AND BATTLEFIELD
314 WEST MAIN STREET
LOUISA, VA 23093
434-589-8989 OR 540-967-1832
WWW.TREVILIANSTATION.ORG

JERDONE'S CASTLE

Front entrance to Jerdone's Castle

Hailing from Scotland, Francis Jerdone was a merchant who immigrated to Virginia in 1746. He kept a very thriving business, and tobacco made him wealthy. He bought some land in 1752—almost a thousand acres. Currently, only 125 acres can be seen, since the rest is sitting under Lake Anna. He built a house on the property and named it Jerdone Castle (Taylor 1992). It is colonial in style, with two and a half stories. There was also a smaller addition built for his granddaughter, Sarah Jerdone Coleman. Jerdone himself died a very rich man from his many businesses in several states. It was said he had buried his wealth somewhere on the property, but it has never been found (Virginia Historic Landmark n.d.).

A woman who used to live in the house described it as being eerie. The spiral and winding staircases are covered in cobwebs, and the dungeon-like cellar gives a historical familiarity with Jerdone's time. Jack Deaton, one of the current owners, told a story about seeing lights coming down the driveway at night—getting closer and closer to the house. They would suddenly vanish into thin air, leaving the people watching out the windows to wonder what happened (Taylor 1992).

There is a ghost in residence. It is allegedly Francis Jerdone's wife, Sara. She also likes to open and close wardrobe closets in the rooms. Interestingly enough, a famous Virginia writer, Ellen Glasgow, lived at Jerdone's Castle for nine years; she is reported to haunt her house in Richmond, Virginia, on Main Street. George Washington also spent several nights in Jerdone Castle when traveling (Taylor 1992).

JERDONE CASTLE
1179 MOODY TOWN ROAD
BUMPASS, VA 23024
PRIVATE RESIDENCE

SPRING GROVE MEMORIAL CEMETERY

Found on Route 522 in Mineral, Virginia, this cemetery is different from most. The stones are gorgeous works of art. As you explore this cemetery, you will notice that a multitude of young people are buried here. Many of the stones I saw were for people who had died at thirty years and younger. I found this to be heartbreaking; we hate to lose our loved ones at any age, but being younger makes it even worse.

This is a place for ghosts to be seen. There is a spirit woman who walks up and down the road in front of the cemetery at different intervals. A visitor in the cemetery that day told me about how she always wears black. As soon as she gets to one side

Road where a spirit lady has been seen walking in front of cemetery

The resting place of the gentleman who wanted his grave cleaned

of the grounds, she vanishes. Reportedly, at dusk there are people seen in the back of the cemetery. However, these reports have never been substantiated.

I had a peculiar event take place while I was visiting the location. I was walking through, taking pictures of the artistic stones, when I was pulled to a specific grave. I stood there and looked down at the site to see what was wrong. I am one of those people who will go through a cemetery and replace flowers back in their holders. It is just my small way of helping.

I took a few pictures, moved to the next grave, and was pulled back again. This time, I took an extra look around and saw that his footstone was completely covered with grass. I leaned down to clear it off for him, stood back up, and was able to move away from the gravesite. I guess he just wanted people to be able to see his name clearly.

It is these types of experience that prove to me that the dead are still with us, and they still have their own unique personalities. I love it when this kind of thing happens, giving me a brief window into the veil.

SPRING GROVE MEMORIAL PARK CEMETERY
2779 PENDLETON ROAD
MINERAL, VA 23117
540-894-5100

COUNTRY WAY STORE

My brother and I were on the way to Louisa Courthouse when we saw this old place, so we stopped to take a few photos. A woman in the house next to the Country Way Store told us some interesting stories about the site. She stated she had bought many of her clothes from the store. The store had only two owners the whole time it was in business.

Back in December 2016, the house sitting beside the store burned down. Other tragedies have occurred around the store as well. Four horses that lived in the barn behind the store all were killed one night by the same lightning strike. Their saddles can still be found sitting in the barn, waiting for their turn to be useful again. Another horse was in the pasture drinking water from the half-frozen pond and

Country Way Store

fell through the ice. Another lady saw what happened and wrangled the horse out of the water and back to the barn. As they walked, a huge branch fell on both the horse and the woman and killed them.

Coincidentally, the current neighbor in the back pasture has a white horse that roams the pasture with no issues at all. The location has old country charm and a sad and haunting past. It is hoped that someone will revitalize the store and bring it back to its former glory one day.

COUNTRY WAY STORE
ROUTE 208, 3059 COURTHOUSE ROAD
LOUISA, VA 23093

HAWKWOOD

Built in 1851 by Alexander Jackson Davis, Hawkwood resembles an Italian villa. Stuccoed brick forms a two-story type of villa with roof wings on both sides. The entry hall is octagonal in shape, and there is a three-story tower on the south wing of the house. Unfortunately, in 1982 a massive fire damaged most of the house. The walls and towers are still standing, and the house has been placed on the Register of Historic Places in Virginia (Louisa County 2015).

Susan Jofko and her roommate moved into the beautiful home in the 1970s. Almost immediately, they were plagued with strange and unusual occurrences. At night, they would hear people walking across the floors. Susan remembers explicitly the sound of shoe soles hitting the floorboards. When she ran out of her room one night to see who it could possibly be, there was no one there (Taylor 1992).

Another evening, both roommates could hear cabinets in several rooms opening and closing, as if someone was searching for something. When they approached the kitchen to see who was causing the racket, no one was discovered, and the cabinet doors were shut. They would also hear the sound of a flute every so often that would start with a very low tune and slowly get higher. Many friends who came to visit Susan and her roommate asked about these happenings (Taylor 1992).

One night after dinner, Susan and her friends began to talk about the "ghost" that lived in the house with them. One of her male friends stated he didn't believe that ghosts existed. At that precise moment, the living-room door that had been locked shut unlatched itself and swung wide open. The door then returned to its closed position and latched the lock back by itself. No one knew what to think after that (Taylor 1992).

Susan had a Rhodesian ridgeback that would watch something or someone walk back and forth in the house. The dog would growl and act like something was in the room, but Susan never saw anything. One night when she was alone, one of the back doors opened on its own like someone was coming in for the night. After that, it swung shut and firmly closed against the doorjamb. As Susan and a friend were outside looking at a specific window in the house, they thought they saw a man's shadow on the other side of the window. Of course, when she went to see who it could be, no one was found. She has no explanation for the strange occurrences but says that she would be very disappointed to find out it wasn't a ghost after all (Taylor 1992).

HAWKWOOD
SOUTH OF GORDONSVILLE OFF ROUTE 15
LOUISA, VA 23093
540-967-0096, 540-693-3200 EXTENSION 1020, 540-371-1112

FLUVANNA

OAKLAND FARM AND SCHOOL

Founded by Margaret Shepherd in 1950, Oakland School educates children with learning disabilities who living in central Virginia. She started the school on her family's farm during the summers to assist those students who needed extra help in their studies. She promoted positive reinforcement and a very nurturing environment. In 1967, she created a program that ran year-round. She took all students, male or female, and loved working with those who were the most challenging to teach (Oakland School 2017b).

Oakland School

Oakland is located in Keswick, and the property is centered on a big house that has been around since before the American Revolution. Built in the 1700s, it is now the home of many classrooms and some administrative offices. There are many gardens to enjoy, and one has a gazebo that claims the best spot for reflecting, studying, or reading. To further their development, a nearby stable is home to a few horses to teach the students how to care for them (Oakland School 2017a).

Strange occurrences have been taking place at the school since Margaret Shepherd moved into the facility. Many people have heard doors slamming, loud parties, footsteps, and even sleigh bells ringing. Loud voices with British accents are heard in the kitchen, along with the tossing of pots and pans. When a teacher checked the kitchen, no one was seen. They have also found many types of orbs in photographs taken around the property (Sancken 2010).

Another story concerns an electrician installing fixtures in the attic. He left dust on the floor after completing his work on the wall. The next morning, large footprints were scattered through the dust (Sancken 2010). The electrician may have made them himself, but these prints were bare feet (Taylor 1992). The footprints reappeared a couple of weeks later, accompanied by a set of smaller ones. Now every spring, they both appear together in the attic. Investigators and a medium visited the facility and found two spirits: a little girl and her nanny. Apparently, they discovered that the girl had died of diphtheria at the age of seven (Sancken 2010).

One more story that really illustrates the strange happenings at the school concerns a student who drowned in the ocean at Virginia Beach. A faculty member saw him one night after he died; the instructor was convinced it was the dead boy because he was large for his age and had a Caesar-like haircut and a Roman type of nose. The instructor couldn't see through the figure; however, he also didn't think it was a real person standing there (Taylor 1992).

OAKLAND SCHOOL
128 OAKLAND WAY
TROY, VA 22974

TROY'S MARKET & DELI

My brother found this location when he searching for another site. The people inside, Liz and Joe Konan as well as their friend, Mandy, were quite welcoming and helpful. Liz told me she was drawn to the location, as are many people who come

Troy's Market & Deli

to the market. They also have a small dinette, Penne Lane, where you can go and enjoy different sandwiches and sides.

The two people who own the establishment, Joe and Elizabeth, are chefs who have worked at some very upscale restaurants and hotels. While training at a French culinary school, Joe learned under the tutelage of Julia Child. The first store Joe and Elizabeth started was in 2003, before they found the Troy location. The talk of the neighborhood is their cookie selection and their almond chicken. They have a great assortment of meals, sandwiches, and other delectable goodies, and they can also help you plan for your next meeting or special occasion (Penne Lane Caterers 2011).

It used to be the family home for Liz's grandmother, who died there at age ninety-seven. The location was also said to be a makeshift hospital in the Civil War (Konan 2016).

Dinette area where I felt a strong presence

One day, a two-year-old boy came with his dad and kept going to the backroom. They could hear the child speaking to someone in his limited language. They found him and brought him back to his dad. The staff also shut the door so he wouldn't get hurt. When they asked him whom he was talking to, he stated that his friends were here and not to worry. He also kept smiling and making circles with his hands (Konan 2016).

When I visited the location, the owners let me walk through the building. I was pulled to a spot in the middle of the dinette, and I asked Liz what this was. She said she thought her grandmother had lived in the space, and there may have been a wall in that spot. She thought her grandmother still hung around the market, since she could feel her presence at different intervals. There was also a strong pull in the kitchen area. Her grandmother had her bedroom in this area as well.

TROY'S MARKET & DELI
19321 JAMES MADISON HIGHWAY
TROY, VA 22974
434-589-4444
HTTP://PENNELANE-TROYMARKET.COM/

FORK UNION MILITARY ACADEMY

Fork Union Military Academy front gate

Fork Union Military Academy (FUMA), founded by Dr. William Hatcher in 1898, started its classes with nineteen boys and girls. Military structure and disciplines were added in 1902 to help the students become better organizers and develop their physical prowess. By 1913, the school had switched over to an all-male student body. Their guiding principles and core values have not changed since the school began. The core values include respect, integrity, faith, character, and discipline (Fork Union Military Academy n.d.).

The school itself is part of the Baptist General Association and has programs for grades 7–12. Classes are taken one at a time instead of the usual six to seven classes in a day. This allows the students to focus on the subject and learn more efficiently, rather than incorporating six different subjects at once. They have supervised study times, punishments for rules broken or cheating, and inspections of the students' rooms daily to ensure cleanliness and organization of clothing and materials at all times (Fork Union Military Academy n.d.).

Some of the buildings on the property are known to be haunted. The first one, Hatcher Hall, is named for the founder himself. The hall houses the administration offices and some of the liberal arts classes (Fork Union Military Academy n.d.). Hatcher built the residence and lived there until he died in 1912. His daughter never wanted to rearrange or touch his living quarters. Dr. Hatcher still roams his old study; sometimes, he is seen in an upstairs window at the residence, within a glowing fog. Whistling has been heard as well as feet shuffling down the hallway (Hauck 2002). Many of the students and faculty say that when they are in Hatcher Hall, it feels as if somebody is watching them as they walk down the corridor. There are reports of doors slamming, especially after curfew hours. Whenever someone goes to check out the noise, they don't find anyone (Ghosts of America n.d.i). Another time, some students switched off all the lights in the whole building. After turning down one hallway, they heard footsteps behind them in the dark. After they went downstairs, the footsteps still echoed on the floor above them. A dark entity brushed against them when they made it to the ground floor. Frightened, with no explanations for the occurrences, they bolted to the administrator's office (Ghosts of America n.d.i).

Other places around the campus are haunted as well. In the old infirmary building, footsteps are heard at different intervals. Right under the quartermaster's office, a young girl in a white dress with no eyes has been seen at different times. The chapel has a light near the top that turns off and on by itself. The room where it happens has been locked for many years; no one can get into it. Some footprints were seen in the parade field one day after a heavy snow. It is interesting to note that they started in the middle, not at the beginning of the walkway (Ghosts of America n.d.i).

FORK UNION MILITARY ACADEMY
4744 James Madison Highway
Fluvanna, VA 23055
434-842-3212
www.forkunion.com

Bremo Plantation, Bremo Recess, and Lower Bremo

Located in Bremo Bluff, Virginia, this 1,500-acre property holds three different mansions that were completed at different intervals. The Lower Bremo home was finished in 1725, Bremo Recess in 1812, and Bremo Mansion in 1819. The architecture of the homes was designed by Thomas Jefferson, John Hartwell Cocke, and John Neilson. Lower Bremo and Bremo Recess are of Jacobean style, whereas the Bremo Mansion is in Palladian style. The plantation was declared a National Historic Landmark in 1971, and it has gorgeous views of the James River (LandmarkHunter 2016).

John Hartwell Cocke started construction of the three homes in 1908. He took the name "Bremo" from his family's home in Scotland, called Braemore, and completed the larger house in 1812. His wife, Anne, loved the home; however, she passed away in 1816 and is buried on the property at Bremo Recess. Her ghost is said to wander the house and grounds.

Robert E. Lee and his wife, Mary, stayed at the plantation during the Civil War, when they both were suffering with their own health issues. Thomas Jefferson is said to have visited the property since his own Monticello was similar in design (LandmarkHunter 2016).

Bremo Plantation has its own resident ghost. Many believe it to be the wife of John Hartwell Cocke, Anne Blaws Baraud. She didn't want to leave the beautiful home her husband had built for her, and still wanders through its corridors (Haunted Places 2016a). Someone in Fluvanna told me that people who have lived there also complain about hearing the voices of many people in the lower rooms. When they go to check the rooms, nobody is there. The lights are out, and there is only silence. Another story is about a woman who lived in the house who folded some sheets to take upstairs with her. She walked away and when she came back to get them—they were missing. Thinking she had already placed them on the bed, she tore down the bedspread to see. The missing sheets were not there. She finally asked the house to please give her back her sheets. When she walked into another room a few minutes later, she found the sheets folded nice and neat for her (Ghosts of America n.d.h).

There is also a story about another guest—this time at Bremo Recess. A lady in a green dress approached Dr. Lewis Greene, who was staying alone at the house. He followed her through the house to see what she was after, and she disappeared when she entered the dining area. Dr. Green had an open wine bottle with him. When the lady disappeared, so did his wine (Sancken 2010).

BREMO PLANTATION
PRIVATE RESIDENCE

5.

GOOCHLAND

WALLER GOLD MINE

Having the Virginia Gold-Pyrite Belt running through the state helped secure its claim on gold mining. The belt runs through many counties, including Fairfax, Culpeper, Orange, Spotsylvania, Fluvanna, Goochland, Louisa, and Cumberland. Gold mining in Virginia began in 1804; however, with the advent of the California Gold Rush, many prospectors decided to head west to get their share. The Civil War came in 1861 and promptly halted all mining. The Union troops, anxious to destroy the South's foothold and economy, damaged or destroyed most of the mines they found.

Sitting in close proximity to the Moss Gold Mine and the Payne Tract Mine near Tabscott, the Waller Gold Mine was discovered in 1831. It sits roughly forty miles from Richmond, near the James River (Faust 1936). Known as one of the best gold mines in the country, it was said to have some of the choicest ore ever mined. Many different rocks and minerals were found here, such as pyrite, gold, chalcopyrite, sphalerite, calcite, copper, kyanite, quartz, silver, marcasite, and zircon (Virginia's Rockhounder n.d., Mindat.org 2015).

A tale that accompanied the mine was about the house where employees lived at the time. Every night, there were strange and unusual noises heard from the house. It was reported as haunted in the early 1900s. Cries and wails frightened many people, so they tried to avoid the house altogether. There is an old legend about a gentleman who kept some of the gold he had found in the mine. He had stashed it in a good hiding place inside the house. Another man who lived with him started to wonder if he really was hiding any gold. The man followed the gentleman one day to see if he could discover the hidden location of the gold. Several days later, screams were heard from the gentleman's room. When they rushed to check on him, they discovered him on the floor with his head partially bashed in, possibly from a blunt weapon. He died later that night. The case remained unsolved for many years afterward, and no one ever came forward with clues to solve the case. Waller Mine was closed down after it was felt that everything possible had been reaped (Kinney 2009).

Many years later, the gentleman who killed the first man confessed to the deed. He had met with some bad times and an accident himself. He described how he snuck into the man's room and stepped on a floorboard that made an awful noise, awaking the man in bed. The gentleman swung an axe at the man's head, still on the pillow. After the man screamed, he hurried back out to hide quickly before the other tenants arrived. He later hid the ax by burying it, and he dug up the gold he could find and headed northward, never to return (Kinney 2009).

The man never found peace after he left. The man he killed haunted him horribly, and he could never come to terms with it even after he confessed. They say the noises from the house, the creaking and the screaming, come from the murdered man still trying to find his lost gold (Kinney 2009).

WALLER GOLD MINE
4300 BLOCK OF SHANNON HILL ROAD IN TABSCOTT
PRIVATELY OWNED

THE AUTHOR'S HOME

I wanted to relay a short story about my own home here in Goochland. We have lived here for sixteen years, and we never heard anything until some of our pets passed away. We had one dachshund, Simba, and several cats, including Sandy and Mr. Imp. They all lived to old age—around fourteen to fifteen years old.

After Simba died, we were distraught. She was fifteen and a very sweet pup. About a month after her death, I awoke one morning around 2:00 to hear a noise in the hallway. I got up to see if one of the cats was chasing the other one, but there was nothing there. As I stood there, I heard it again. It sounded like little feet running up and down the hallway. I suddenly thought about Simba, who loved to go ninety miles an hour through the house. I told her to go lie down and be quiet. The noise stopped. She comes to visit once or twice a month, and she still listens to me.

Sandy and Mr. Imp, two cats we lost in 2015 and 2016, respectively, also come back to visit. Sandy used to jump up on the bed and move around until she found a good spot. She would also claw at the door when she wanted to come inside from the cold. After she passed, about two weeks later we heard a scratching at the door. Thinking it was Mr. Imp, we opened the door to find nothing there and discovered

Simba, Sandy, and Mr. Imp

Mr. Imp was inside his cathouse. This went on for several weeks. Recently, we have had other occurrences. After I go to bed, I always feel something jump on the bed and walk around. I got up one night, turned on the light, and saw nothing. I knew it was Sandy, though, and I told her she could stay as long as she wanted. She was a sweet cat and very lovable.

Mr. Imp passed away in November 2016 on my deceased father's birthday. Daddy loved Mr. Imp, so I am glad they are back together again. About a month after Mr. Imp died, we started to smell different odors that we associated with Mr. Imp. Then one day after we noticed a scent, my husband saw some black cat hairs in a chair where the kitty loved to sleep. We told him to come back and visit, too. We miss him terribly.

PROVIDENCE PRESBYTERIAN CHURCH

Having been established in the early 1740s, Providence Presbyterian Church started with a group of people who wanted to read the Bible and worship the Lord at Samuel Morris's home. Many people heard about the services and began attending. As the small group grew, Samuel started to build more meeting places to house them all. The governor at the time allowed them to worship under the Act of Toleration.

Samuel Davies also came in 1747 to minister to the growing congregation. It is often stated that Patrick Henry was greatly influenced by Davies's skill both as an orator and a leader. He taught many slaves how to read during his tenure, and he also sent forth help for the Native Americans on the land (Providence Presbyterian Church n.d.).

John Todd became the congregation's first pastor in 1752 and remained until 1793, when he died. He lived in Louisa and was a supporter of the American Revolution. He began one of the first classical schools, which became the blueprint for Hampden-Sydney College.

As with any church congregation, the attendance waxed and waned over many years. The congregation was almost wiped out due to heavy battles and enlistment of soldiers during the Civil War. At any given time, there were always a few members in the area, and the usual congregation consisted of about forty people (Providence Presbyterian Church n.d.).

With population increase and the completion of Interstate 64, Providence began to grow by leaps and bounds. They built a new educational building in 1986 where they have a preschool and Vacation Bible School. The preschool operates each weekday, and the Bible school hosts sixty-plus children every year (Providence Presbyterian Church n.d.).

The church has some interesting ghost stories in its history. A woman who used to go with her grandmother to clean the church states that she never felt comfortable there. She would get eerie feelings whenever she journeyed onto the balcony or in

Providence Presbyterian Church

a small side room. She was once sitting in the car when she glanced at one of the balcony windows. She spotted a young girl in a bright-yellow dress with white spots and a white collar. As soon as she tried to get a better look, the young girl disappeared. After that, she always had the feeling of being watched whenever she was in the church, but she never went back alone again (Ghosts of America n.d.e).

When I visited the church, I ran into two nice ladies, Teresa and Ms. Epps, who told me they had not heard about the particular haunting at the church. They were very helpful and let me take pictures of the interior and exterior of the church. There were two markers in the front for the two ministers mentioned above, Samuel Davies and John Todd. I did a recording session, but I did not get any sounds or voices. I did get an eerie feeling of being watched every so often. It was not a malevolent feeling, just a curious one. As I moved back toward the playground, I noticed the swings moving back and forth as if someone was riding them. The wind was blowing on this day, but I don't know if it was strong enough to move one swing, then the other. It was like there were two people starting at different times. Very interesting to watch, but as I stated, it could have been the wind.

PROVIDENCE PRESBYTERIAN CHURCH
3388 THREE CHOPT ROAD
GUM SPRING, VA 23065
804-556-6327
HTTPS://PROVIDENCEPC.WORDPRESS.COM

CASTELLO HOUSE

I visited Paige and Steven on a gorgeous Saturday afternoon when the temperatures were in the 70s. Paige is also a nurse, so we had much in common. I enjoyed listening to stories from her job and telling her about working in the operating room. Steven also joined us for the tour and told me about the spoiled pups who were taking over the sofa beside me.

As we got to talking about the house, I specifically asked Paige not to tell me anything, since I did not want anything she said to influence what I felt. We decided to just walk through and see what I sensed in each room of the house. Starting in the front room, I started to feel something over by the large piano. Paige stated that they can usually tell if something is present by the way the house feels when they walk in the front door (Castello 2017).

When I told her about the specific spot, it felt like I was being pushed up against a wall. I was also getting a little cold at the time. We headed toward the office and the back bedroom, and I turned around to take a few pictures of the spot. I saw a quick white shimmer at the end of the hallway, but I did not mention it to Paige or Steven as I had new glasses and hadn't gotten used to them yet. I figured my eyes were playing tricks on me.

In the back office, I started to get extremely cold. My teeth even started to chatter as if it were ice cold in the room. There was also a very heavy feeling in the room; I felt a very strong presence as well. Paige said everything started in this room. She said she felt like it was something bad, but it was not present all the time.

I did not feel anything malevolent myself; however, I did feel a very strong entity. I asked if they knew any of the history of the home or the land. There was a plantation in the back of the house. Although when Paige and Steven moved in, there were only pines all over the property and before that, the land held hay fields as far as the eye could see. They have found many arrowheads all over the property leading me to ask about Native American grounds or settlements. They did not know of any at present (Castello 2017).

We left the office and walked across the hall to the bedroom. I also felt a presence in this room, but it was not as strong as the one in the office. Paige told me about some of the weird happenings in this room. The pictures tilt sideways and the closet door, which clicks into place, opens by itself.

The bathroom between the office and the bedroom also has a ghostly visitor at times. I did not get anything in the bathroom, but Paige told me that she could close the shower curtain and go back a few days later, and it would be half open. If she fixed it, a few days later, it would be open again. Paige also told me about her son being locked in the bathroom by "something," which is strange in itself as the lock is on the inside of the door (Castello and Castello 2017).

I went back to the office after exiting the bathroom for another look. This room really piqued my interest. I wanted to see if I got the same heavy feelings again. The room was very heavy and cold. Paige told me that sometimes both she and Steven have seen a dark figure with no real shape in the room. It isn't there all the time, but when it is, you will know it. She doesn't like to spend much time in the room at all. Steven uses the room as an office, I asked him about his feelings toward it. He stated he wasn't scared, but he sometimes felt very nervous about the presence.

They did have Transcend Paranormal come out and investigate the occurrences. They told them that the stronger presence was in the back bedroom rather than the office. They felt that there was a negative force only in the office at the time. Their EMF readers were going off, and they were getting many different readings (Castello and Castello 2017).

One of the Transcend Paranormal group also asked if he had cows in his yard. Unbeknown to the group member, Steven had raised cattle in the past on his property. She saw one out the window, by the fence. There have been no cows on the property for a long time. Another member saw a German shepherd dog walking across the front yard that had passed away some years ago.

All of this led me to ask when the occurrences started. Steven told me they moved to the house in 2004 after he spent two years building their dream home. His dad became sick after suffering from dementia, so they brought him to live with them so they could take care of him. He passed away three days later in the back bedroom. Steven described his father as mean at times due to the dementia. It was quite a battle to get him to move to Virginia from Florida so they could look after him.

After his father's death, all the weird phenomena started happening. Steven came home one day to find all the smoke detectors hanging down from the top pieces. These are the kind of detectors where you screw the bottom piece into the top. He went through the house and fixed them all. Forty-eight hours later, they all were out again. He leaves them hanging down at present, since they will not stay attached. He even tried changing the wiring, to no avail (Castello and Castello 2017).

Another day, he came home to find the large piano in the front room moved about eight inches from the wall. A picture on top was even leaning between the piano and the wall. This is a very heavy piece of furniture; you cannot move it easily. They could find no logical explanation for the movement. I asked about earthquakes or other phenomena around that time, but they said nothing had happened out of the ordinary as far as weather or earthquakes. Steven also told me that Transcend Paranormal noted a big change right in front of the piano, about where I said there was an issue.

Steven thinks some of the happenings are a manifestation of his father still holding on to them. After his father's death, things also started to progress further. His mother became sick a few years later and came to stay with them. She moved into a bedroom on the other side of the house, where she passed away.

Around this time, Steven started seeing a shimmer at the end of the hallway and by his mother's room. It was exactly where I had also seen the shimmer a few minutes before, while he was talking to me in same place. I thought it was me, but I saw the shimmer twice. The shimmers started right before his mother died. Was it family coming to meet her?

When Steven's mother died, Paige saw a lady walk across the front room, wearing a long dress similar to those from the 1800s. She was kicking up the back of the

Piano that moved by itself, and hallway with shimmer seen at far end

dress as she walked. Then she suddenly disappeared off the other side of the front room (Castello and Castello 2017).

A few days after his mother passed, things started to calm down, and they thought maybe his father had left with his mother. Most of last summer, nothing happened in the house. Steven told Paige that maybe there wasn't anything in the house anymore. He had said it a couple times, in fact.

On one of those nights, while cooking their dinner and talking about the lack of activity, the bottom left kitchen window shattered above the sink. Twelve hours later, the right one shattered. These windows were made of two panes of glass, one inside and one outside. The strange thing here was that only the inside pane shattered on both windows. No breaking pattern could be found either; it was just smashed outright (Castello and Castello 2017).

Both Steven and Paige took it as a message that the house was not empty, and that there still may be a presence lurking. As we chatted about the happenings in the house, we debated how many entities were present. They had one they considered malevolent in the back office, and there were at least three others that seem more mischievous in nature. For example, the slanting pictures in three different rooms seem to say, "I am here; pay attention to me."

They both thought it had something to do with the house itself. Both of Steven's parents died in the house, so could this be an explanation? They also discovered that the Miller Plantation was located on the property many years ago. Could something have happened on the grounds, causing the manifestations? A third idea was the number of arrowheads found in the soil around the house and all over the property. Could this have been a Native American reservation or living space? I also explained that sometimes it was not just the house, but the land itself that leads to the manifestation of spirits. I suggested researching Miller Plantation and the surrounding land to see if any events may have led to these occurrences. Transcend Paranormal brought historical land maps with them to show where the plantation may have sat on the property (Castello and Castello 2017).

For a long time, they believed that the entities were playful; then it began to turn darker. They would walk in the house and feel something was not right. Their friends who visit even say the house feels weird at times. Some refuse to stay in the back bedroom or use the office space. One of their nonbeliever friends admitted that his

Kitchen windows that broke
from the inside only

Pictures hanging crooked
in the living room

deceased uncle came to see him when he stayed in the back bedroom. The man described his uncle as solid and being able to touch him.

We decided to check out Steven's mom's room on the other side of the house. On the way, Paige said they always heard a noise in the hallway that sounded like a golf ball dropping on the floor and rolling across it, but nothing is ever found upon inspection.

There was a light presence in the room, and I would almost describe it as kind and sweet. The pictures in this room are doilies that have been framed, and they tilt like all the other pictures in the home. There is also a closet door that clicks tightly shut, but it will open by itself on occasion.

We moved on to Paige and Steven's bedroom, which is painted in a gorgeous red color. Steven told me of a couple of nights before, when he noticed his dog looking toward the fireplace and growling. When he investigated, he saw nothing out of the ordinary. (Castello and Castello 2017). As I walked around the room, I stopped in front of the fireplace and near the back windows. The feeling had gone from light to heavy when moving toward the fireplace. I didn't get cold, but I did sense this was a welcoming entity.

For a long time, Steven thought his dad was still at the house after his death. When I asked him how he handled this situation, he told me he began to talk to his dad each day. He felt that it was helpful and made him feel better each time. He also described a time when the Transcend Paranormal group was in the back bedroom and asking questions. He went and stood in the doorway just to listen. They asked if the entity knew who was standing in the doorway to the room at that moment.

They received no answer at first, so they headed back to the living room. As they got to the kitchen, an answer of SON came across their box. This was the first proof Steven had of his dad still being in the home.

Another interesting thing to note about this property is an old building across the road from the gravel driveway. One day, Steven had gone out to take some pictures of the structure, and as he got closer, he saw a yellow flash travel across the front of the building. He couldn't figure out what it was, but he figured it just did not want to have its picture taken that day (Castello and Castello 2017).

This house has some very interesting occurrences, and I researched Miller Plantation just to see what I could find. Sadly, I have found nothing yet, but I am going to continue looking because I would like to see what happened on the land to cause these things to occur.

PAIGE AND STEVEN CASTELLO
PRIVATE RESIDENCE

GRAYHAVEN WINERY

I visited this charming vineyard on a crisp Sunday morning to meet the owners, Max and Deon, chat with them about the winery, and hear some of the ghostly tales. The animals—three dogs and two horses—all roam the property. There is also a koi pond as you cross the bridge leading to the tasting room, with some gorgeous fish in it. Ask about Daisy, since the pup does love to talk and tell her stories.

The land itself was part of a 1917 land grant that was awarded to the Isbell family. Some members of the family are still on the property in the original graveyard up near the road. There is a slave graveyard on another part of the property. While exploring the vineyard, Max and her family have discovered arrowheads and many Civil War artifacts (Abrams and Abrams 2016).

Grayhaven was founded by Max's parents, Lyn and Chuck Peple, in 1978. They were no relation to the Isbell family, but they were looking for some real estate with the right type of soil for growing a vineyard. It was a retirement venture for the family that quickly grew into a steady business. Grayhaven Winery started producing their unique wines in 1994. They produce many different styles, such as sauvignon blanc, cabernet, Traminette, and Pinotage. They also have wines in red, white, and blush styles (Grayhaven Winery 2009). They were one of six wineries in Virginia starting out in 1978. In 1980, they harvested their first grapes. In comparison, there are over 275 wineries in Virginia today (Abrams and Abrams 2016).

Deon stated that many paranormal groups have come and investigated the vineyard and declared it a superhighway for ghosts. They brought cameras, voice recorders, and pendulums to discern different energies. He also told me about Three Chopt Trail, which used to run alongside the creek that surrounds the property (Owens Creek), and in one area, there is a huge drop-off where many stagecoaches fell into the creek. Many spirits inhabit in this spot.

Another story Deon related had to do with the paranormal group investigating the slave graveyard on the land. You can see many stones and depressions in this graveyard. When questioned, Deon told the investigator that there were six graves in the area. The investigator stated there were instead sixteen. When Deon asked how he knew this, the investigator stated that one of the dead people had told him the information.

They called members from the original family a couple of months later to help them clean up the gravesites in the slave graveyard. One of the older family members brought a pile of family papers with him, which contained a will left from a father to a son. A particular slave had been mentioned in the will, and the slave's name was the same as one the investigator had been speaking to in the graveyard (Abrams and Abrams 2016).

While my husband enjoyed the mulled spice wine in the tasting room, Deon gave me directions to find the family cemetery right down from the parking lot. It sits overlooking the vineyard and is near the road. As I walked among the stones, I felt some strange push-pull sensations and just some weird eerie feelings. I did get the feeling of being watched a couple of times; however, I did not feel unsafe.

The first stone you will see is that of William E. Isbell. He was born in 1837 and served in the 44th Virginia Infantry Regiment in Company A in addition to the 20th Virginia Heavy Artillery Battalion. He wrote many letters to family and friends during his time in the military. He wrote to his sister, Anna, and told her of leading some soldiers through a town and raiding the establishments that sold alcohol. He spoke of his encampments during the war and how the weather was brutally cold at times. He also described the many snowball fights they had in Highland County

Grayhaven Tasting Room

125

Grayhaven Family Graveyard

at Camp Johnson. He died in 1924 and was buried here at his family home (Find A Grave n.d.).

Some of the other stones indicate other family members. The list includes William Reid Isbell, George W Isbell, Bernard Louis Isbell, Ophelia Mayo Isbell, Benjamin Wallace Isbell, Thomas Isbell (lived for only one month), and Sarah Letitia Mayo Isbell. There are also three stones at the foot of the cemetery, but the Abramses were not sure if these were headstones or the footstones from other graves. There is also one stone under a nearby bush that has broken apart, and it is hard to tell anything about it at present.

After my visit to the family graveyard, I headed back to the tasting room as Deon was cooking some of their famous mulled wine. If you get a chance, you must try this wonderful wine. It is very warming on a chilly day, with a fine, rich flavor and a relaxing aroma. I do not typically like red wine at all, but I love this particular brew. I met up with Max on the way back, and we chatted about the other locations I wanted to visit on the property. After my husband and I finished our wine, we headed out to see the slave graveyard with Max. She reiterated about the land grant in 1917 and how the land had passed hands through the years (Abrams and Abrams 2016).

Currently, Max is trying to identify the slaves who are buried on the property. The Isbell family had placed the slave graveyard on the other side of the property from their own family graveyard. There are at least six stones and many deep depressions in the area. Max, Deon, and other family members have kept this small graveyard cleaned up and maintained for many years. Max believes that it is a very peaceful place, since it feels like the spirits here have moved on and left a very positive energy (Abrams and Abrams 2016).

Slave graveyard, with Daisy leading the way

Max told us a story about her and her sister wandering in the woods one day in 1978. They stopped about 200 yards from the slave graveyard with their Ouija® board. The board had a spirit attached to it named Ralph. The board never worked properly, so both sisters thought the other one actually was moving the planchette whenever the board spoke. They found out that Ralph had perished in a car accident with his girlfriend, and he had never really gotten past the guilt. They spoke to him on and off for several years, but when they brought the board to the slave graveyard, Ralph quickly told them that he couldn't come to the graveyard. That was the last time they heard from him, and the board never worked again (Abrams and Abrams 2016).

She has had many energy-related things happen on the property as well. One day, Max was in an old part of the house, built in 1910. She was sitting on a bed, which started to shake. The next thing she knew, she felt like she was floating toward the ceiling, with the rough wood rubbing the side of her face. She was too scared to open her eyes to see what was happening. Another time, she was walking through the old part of her house, and she turned around and happened to glance in the mirror in front of her. Everything in the reflection was green; however, there was no green in the room behind her, nor was she wearing anything green in color. She did state that there were cold patches throughout the house even in the summer. She has felt something or someone following her through the house (Abrams and Abrams 2016).

After we left the slave graveyard, we headed to the "Magic Spot." Max described it as having many spirits of animals around you. It is set on a beautiful hill overlooking the creek and another part of the property.

As we carefully made our way there, her three dogs frolicked in the cold water of the creek and followed along behind us. The nice thing about the trails at

Grayhaven is that you can enjoy a glass of wine while you are walking your dog. On this particular day, both Michael and I had a glass of the mulled spice wine with us while we were traveling to each location.

Max told us how the beautiful ivy we saw growing on the trees was still quite green, even though it was November. The ivy was indicative of a settlement having been here in the past, since English ivy is not native to the area. The Isbells and their slaves lived here, but there were also freed ex-slaves who made their home in the area. They were blacksmiths or tradesman who had their businesses or dwellings in this specific location (Abrams and Abrams 2016).

Another interesting sight was the hills that look like they have been cut into; looking down from those, you would see ruts in the ground. Max explained that these were the paths that the carriages or wagons would travel on their way in and out of the property (Abrams and Abrams 2016).

We finally made it to the Magic Spot. It is a very peaceful place that Max and Deon found one day while they were out walking. Max uses it for thinking, writing, or just enjoying the gorgeous view it affords the person who is standing at the edge of the drop-off. Owens Creek runs around the Magic Spot. You could just bring a chair and commune with nature here. It really is a very relaxing place.

As we made our way back to the tasting room, we spoke of the beautiful surroundings and asked Max more about the wine business. It could take up to five years depending on the soil, weather, grape varieties, and deer damage to produce your first bottle of wine. They normally clip the grapes off the vine the first year, since they want all the plant's energy focused on growing strong roots. They also will graft American vines onto other types to make them more hardy. A French hybrid will lead to richer flavors, such as a cabernet. Much of growing grapes is really just trial and error to see what works and what doesn't. A lot of patience and a lot of work go into creating a gorgeous vineyard and great wine (Abrams and Abrams 2016).

Grayhaven Winery uses a special Howard press to help with the grapes each season. This press is one of only five in the United States, and it was brought here in the 1970s. This particular press can press one ton of grapes in a half to three-quarters of a day. In case you were wondering about the remaining smashed grape pulp—like I was—it goes to pig farmers to feed their animals (Abrams and Abrams 2016).

We left a short time later with three bottles of Deon's South African wine and a special mulling packet that adds so many wonderful flavors after being cooked in a crock pot. It also lends a nice smell to your home. I cannot wait to visit again to see what new flavors they have developed.

GRAYHAVEN WINERY
4675 EAST GREY FOX CIRCLE
GUM SPRING, VA 23065
804-556-3917
WWW.GRAYHAVENWINERY.COM

BARN BESIDE OILVILLE POST OFFICE

Barn beside Oilville Post Office

I read about this barn on the Ghosts of America website. It sits just east of the Oilville Post Office, and it does look very foreboding. I asked around in the area to find out if anyone knew any stories or had seen anything in or around the barn. One lady told me she heard shrieks and screams on different occasions. A man said he saw a shadowy figure around the barn late at night, but he was unsure if it was human. If the barn is not haunted, the ghosts are missing a good chance here.

I visited with my brother to take pictures during the day, did not see anything strange, and didn't get anything unusual in our pictures. The barn has an eerie feeling to it. Could the wind be making the noises locals hear?

BARN BESIDE OILVILLE POST OFFICE
EAST OF 1411 BROAD STREET ROAD, ALMOST ACROSS FROM CAR WASH
OILVILLE, VA 23139

NORTH POLE

Established in 1979, the North Pole was known for steaks, seafood, and great meals every night. Located in Crozier, the restaurant was a hotspot for many people coming from different counties, such as Goochland, Henrico, Louisa, and Albemarle. It sits on an acre of land just west of Cardwell Road, and the building was built in 1924 (Hester 2007).

North Pole
Restaurant

Dick Rossi, owner of the North Pole, decided to put the restaurant up for sale in 2007. He wanted to move on and try other things, since he was sixty-seven at the time and just couldn't physically handle running the popular eatery any longer. He was grateful for all the friends and acquaintances who made the restaurant a big success for him over the years. Mr. Rossi passed away in a tragic car accident in 2010. Currently, the restaurant is still for sale.

The North Pole has actually been around since 1924, starting out as an ice cream parlor known as the North Pole Confectionary. It could hold around twenty customers, and they served a lunch menu. When Rossi bought it, he changed the whole premise to that of a restaurant, serving a grand dinner. He enlarged the seating area to hold around one hundred people, and he specialized in seafood and steak dishes. He also employed Steve Bassett to come and entertain people with his musical showcase (Hester 2007).

When I visited the North Pole, I was enchanted by the polar bears in the front of the restaurant. These iconic statues are still standing guard, waiting for hungry patrons to grace the property once more. I had heard stories by several people of a figure in white behind the restaurant, as well as finding one story on the internet (Ghosts of America n.d.d). The figure apparently would sit in the field for hours at a time, then get up and swiftly disappear. One person I talked with tried to get pictures of the figure, but to no avail. It was just too fast. She went back that night to try again, but the figure did not reappear.

Does the figure have something to do with the restaurant or perhaps an event around the property from long ago? Could it be a real person just acting like a ghostly figure?

NORTH POLE
1588 RIVER ROAD WEST
CROZIER, VA 23039

CONWAY'S TOMBSTONE

Conway Cocke's tombstone

Off in a field near an abandoned restaurant on Route 6 in Crozier stands a memorial to a little boy who died at six years old in April 1859. His name was Conway Clifton Cocke. You will not see the grave from the road; you have to get out and walk across the field to find it. It is a regular gravestone that looks like it has been repaired several times, but you can still make out the writing. It is a sad memorial to see, but it is nice to know that the little boy's grave is still around for those like me who wanted to find it. The people who own the property make sure to keep it well tended and clear of debris.

There have been reports of shadows in the field behind the grave, as well as people getting voices on recording devices. One such recording mentions actually hearing the name Conway spoken, even though no one was with them that day (Ghosts of America n.d.d) Is the little boy looking for someone to play with him? Or maybe he is searching for his parents.

CONWAY'S TOMBSTONE
PRIVATE RESIDENCE

CHESTNUT HILL
(PLYNLIMMON)

Chestnut Hill is located in one of the common areas known for ghosts in Goochland. Named for all the chestnut trees growing around the property, it is halfway between the Plynlimmon property and Mount Bernard. There is a huge black rock that marks this point. This is where the ghosts also like to cause mischief. After sundown, visitors may see all kinds of strange things. For example, one person stopped to rest at the rock on the way to Chestnut Hill and heard horses coming up the road toward the rock. After a short wait, no human or animal was ever seen (Richmond 2015).

The house was owned by Judge Isaac Pleasants and his wife, Anne Eliza. Both are buried on the property near Plynlimmon House. Plynlimmon House was also known for having a headless ghost in a white gown who carried a lamp and walked up and down the stairway. She was famous for waiting for everyone to retire at night, walking halfway down the steps, throwing the lamp away, and then throwing herself down the rest of the stairs. There was always a high scream whenever this occurred, even thought the ghost was headless. One brave soul wanted to witness the apparition, so he spent the night at the ghostly abode. The lady showed up and promptly fell down the stairs. The man swore there was fresh blood covering some of the stairs, but no one believed his tale (Richmond 2015).

There was also a story about a big black dog that stayed down near the bottom of Chestnut Hill. He liked to run beside horses or the carriages they were leading. Some people wondered about the dog and decided he may be dangerous, so they tried to shoot him on several occasions. Apparently, the bullets passed right through him as he kept running to keep up with them. They finally came to accept him, and one lawyer who walked to the State Farm to catch a train would often have this black apparition walk beside him all the way home in the dark. He rather liked the companionship and enjoyed the dog's presence (Richmond 2015).

CHESTNUT HILL (PLYNLIMMON)
1 MILE EAST OF MAIDENS ROAD PAST MT. BERNARD
GOOCHLAND, VA 23063

TUCKAHOE PLANTATION

As you make your way down the driveway to the plantation house, you will see a line of trees that seem to stretch on for miles, and many cows in the pasture to greet you to the farm. It almost seems as if you are stepping into plantation life in the 1800s. The house itself is sitting front and center at the end of the driveway, in the shape of a huge H, following early Georgian-type architecture. The plantation also boasts three slave quarters to the right of the house, a majestic memorial garden to the left, and a smokehouse, kitchen, and schoolhouse.

A noted National Historic Landmark, Tuckahoe Plantation was settled in the early 1700s by Thomas Randolph. His son William began construction of the home, which was finally completed by 1740. Since 1733, Tuckahoe has welcomed many notable guests: Robert E. Lee, George Washington, Baron von Clausen, the Comte de Rochambeau, a few Virginia governors, and, more recently, Pierce Brosnan (*Tuckahoe Plantation c. 1733*).

The plantation is rich with history; you can almost imagine a young Thomas Jefferson playing in the large yard or having lessons in the schoolhouse. William Randolph and his best friend, Peter Jefferson, made a pact that if one of them died, the other would take care of his children. As it happened, William died in 1745 at thirty-two, so Peter took his family to Tuckahoe to honor the agreement. It is said that Thomas Jefferson was not quite two years old when the family made the journey from Shadwell to the plantation.

Tuckahoe Plantation main house

The Jeffersons stayed at the plantation for seven years, where all the children attended lessons in the schoolhouse. After the Jeffersons returned to Shadwell in 1752, Thomas Mann Randolph, who was only eleven years old at the time, took over as master of the plantation.

Once he reached adulthood, Thomas Mann married Anne Cary of Ampthill. They had thirteen children, and ten were able to reach adulthood. Anne died on March 16, 1789. This date is etched into one of the glass panes in the White Parlor. Thomas Mann then married Gabriella Harvie, who took to redecorating the house and painted the sitting room all white. It is known today as the "White Parlor." She covered up the Virginia walnut walls with multiple coats of white paint. After Thomas Mann Randolph died in 1795, he was buried on the property in the Randolph Cemetery.

Gabriella Harvie's son, Thomas Mann Randolph III, had an eerie experience in the house. He was suffering from a fever and chills and had not slept most of the night, when he saw a woman coming toward him. She came out of one of the closets beside the large fireplace. She was carrying a tall glass of water, and she told him to drink it and rest. The water revived his spirit, and when he awoke the next day, he was feeling much better and his fever was gone.

Thomas Mann III told his family of the occurrence at breakfast the next day. He swore if he ever found the lady who helped him, he would marry her. After his first wife died, he made a trip to Patterson, New Jersey, for a party. He immediately recognized a blonde woman there named Lucinda Patterson, who resembled the apparition. He asked her to marry him right then, after telling her about the apparition that appeared to him, and she said yes (*Tuckahoe Plantation c. 1733*)

Staircase inside back of house

The current residents live in the basement and second floor of the house, and they enjoy sharing the history with visitors. They are keeping the plantation alive so that future generations can visit where our third president once played and walked the grounds. It is interesting to note that the majority of the buildings are the original structures, and the slave cabins to the right of the house have been remodeled for people living in them today (Sausmikat 2016).

There is a wealth of rich history in this house, with fine woodworking and carvings on staircases and walls. Many stories are told about this house and some of its ghostly visitors. When you step onto the porch, the first thing you notice is the paneling in the door (Thompson 1997). The crosses are said to ward off evil spirits that may try to enter the house. The porch also has a light-blue ceiling to prevent wasps from building nests on it, which may also keep evil spirits away since it is considered a positive color.

As you enter the north doorway, a majestic staircase is to your right. It was carved by a craftsman, probably from England, but the owners are unsure of who he was. The staircase has a twin that once existed at Rosewell Plantation, presumably built by the same craftsman.

To the left is the Burnt Room, which is filled with many paintings of famous people, such as George Washington and "Mad" Anthony Wayne. The ragged flag standing behind the door was originally from the Presidio in San Francisco. In this room's right corner stands a gorgeous cabinet that holds some china pieces and vases. The Grey Lady, who they think is Mary or Judith Randolph, is said to come out of the cabinet every so often. She usually appears to women, but some men have seen her as well. Mary, the unhappy bride, attempted to elope with her true love, but she was brought back by her father until the bishop of London changed his mind. Judith was involved in a scandal in which she allegedly poisoned her husband, Richard Randolph, in 1793.

One time, the residents thought they heard a party in the Burnt Room late at night. They could hear the laughter and glasses clinking, but when they checked to see if someone had broken in, no one was ever found. Apparently, the Grey Lady invited friends over to keep her company. She is both a happy and positive spirit.

The White Parlor, across from the Burnt Room, has its own ghost story. When Pierce Brosnan visited the home to make *The Broken Chain*, there were many Native Americans involved in making the film. They refused to enter the house because they sensed spirits within the boundaries. They called their medicine man, who cleansed the home by using a conch shell with burning herbs and sage. He chanted throughout each room, and when he arrived in the White Parlor, the chandelier started to swing back and forth. This chandelier is made of very heavy glass and crystal, and it is very hard to push or swing for that matter. The windows in the room do not open at all.

After this transpired and the house was fully cleansed, the people saw the spirit of a wolf running through the house. They asked the medicine man if he knew what this meant. He said it meant the house was cleansed and safe now. The Native Americans then felt at ease entering the house to finish the film.

Cabinet where the Grey Lady has been seen

Chandelier from the White Parlor

Vortex Wall on second floor

There is a story about a rocking chair in the Great Hall, which is to the right coming out of the White Parlor. Mary Allen, matriarch of the Allen family, who owned Tuckahoe during the war in the 1860s, kept hearing a voice call her. She was the only one in the house at the time. The voice remained constant, so she finally went to see who was calling out. After she made it upstairs, the roof and ceiling caved in right on top of the chair where she had been sitting. She never found anyone upstairs, but that voice had saved her life.

Once you go upstairs, there is a room to the right called the Red Bedroom due to its red-tinted stained paneling. This room has a large cabinet that is to the left when you walk in the door. There is a wall paneling about halfway down the wall that is said to have a spiritual vortex attached to it. I felt the vibrations at the top of the stairs and asked if any of the rooms were haunted. We went to see the paneling, and I reached out to touch it. I immediately started shaking and got very cold. My brother, who was with me, said he didn't feel anything. Other people have felt vibrations or heard voices when they stand near the panel.

Heading back downstairs, you come into the Great Hall. There is a mirror that hangs on the left wall past the door. It has oxidized over the years, but a photographer took a picture of it when he was visiting the plantation and found something peculiar. The picture contained himself as well as another person, a woman, behind him, facing the mirror. He stated no one else was with him at the time he was taking the pictures. This woman is thought to be the Grey Lady.

Once you walk through the Great Hall, you will come to the Dining Room on the right. In the 1990s, another photographer took a picture of the Grey Lady standing by the dining room table on the right side. You could see the outline of her dress and a blurry face. The interesting thing about the photograph is that today when you see the picture, the Grey Lady is fading while the background of the dining room is intact. Apparently, she was angry at having her picture taken.

In July 1996, the resident and her friend were moving specific items into the attic. The resident was packing some things downstairs while her friend made a trip up to the attic. On the way back across the floor to the steps, the friend was stopped by a curtain of mist that was in her way. There were no windows in the room, so it wasn't a trick of the light. She decided to walk through it and head back downstairs. As soon as she did, she turned ice cold. The resident had to wrap her in warm blankets for a long time to get her warm again.

As you travel outside, you will notice a walkway from the house down to the memorial gardens. The Grey Lady has also been seen on this walkway, called the Ghost Walk (Kinney 2012). There have also been many reports of a young child crying in the gardens or a young girl screaming when no one else was present. It is said that it could be one of the children who perished in the house (Kinney 2012).

There are many legends as well regarding why the lady walks down the Ghost Walk toward the cemetery. One myth is that she is a bride who was left standing at the altar, waiting for her future husband to arrive. Another story is that her true love was killed in the Civil War days before he was supposed to come home and be married. The last story concerns her being forced to marry against her will when she wanted to wait for the soldier to return from war (Brown 2009).

One of the gardeners has spotted the gray fabric of the Grey Lady's dress rush past him when he is working out in the fields and garden areas. He catches it out of the corner of his eye when no one else is present (Steger 2010).

There is one more story that concerns the Grey Lady. This is from a tour guide doing a Christmas tour in December 2015. She was talking to a guest when she saw the Grey Lady in the sitting room, with her heavy skirt moving around her. She says it could have been a trick since the lamp in the room was on, but she had cold chills for a long time after it happened.

The last building outside and to the right of the porch is the schoolhouse where Thomas Jefferson himself attended his lessons, as did other children throughout the house's history, including the current resident's children. The door has a big hole in the bottom of it from centuries of use. There are four or five different locks on the door, as well as many keyholes (Sausmikat 2016).

Are there spirits from the past still living and partying at Tuckahoe Plantation? Go visit and see if you are greeted by one of them.

TUCKAHOE PLANTATION
12601 RIVER ROAD
RICHMOND, VA 23238
804-774-1614 (TOURS)
WWW.TUCKAHOEPLANTATION.COM
TOURS ARE BY APPOINTMENT ONLY. THERE ARE SELF-TOURS OF THE GROUNDS AND GARDENS. BOTH OF THESE COST A NOMINAL FEE. THE GROUNDS ARE OPEN DAILY FROM 9:00 A.M. TO 5:00 P.M., EXCEPT WHEN THERE ARE PRIVATE EVENTS. CHECK THE CALENDAR ON THE WEBSITE FOR SCHEDULING.

6.

POWHATAN/AMELIA

POWHATAN

Sublett's Tavern

SUBLETT'S TAVERN

Sublett's Tavern was built around 1757 and was in use as an "ordinary" or tavern as of 1813. The Sublett family owned the land and property, having received it from the French land patents. Many travelers stopped on their way to Richmond in those days to rest and freshen up before continuing the journey. From 1826 to 1946, the tavern doubled as a post office and a voting counter in the area (Moseley 2016).

I was told of one ghost story surrounding this location in the upstairs bedrooms. There were strange noises, like scratching and knocking at different intervals, and a mist that traveled along the steps. They had no idea what or who it was, but it did scare people who were staying there.

Also in my research, I found a couple who lived in a house next to Sublett's Tavern for a while. They were also having unexplained occurrences. While at a nearby yard sale, they discovered that the people there were previous owners of their home. The previous owners were anxious to know if the current couple had had any strange experiences, such as banging footsteps, whistling, and people talking all over the house. When the previous owners would try to find the cause of these occurrences, they would discover no one else was in the house. They left after living in the home for only a short while (Ghosts of America n.d.g).

SUBLETT'S TAVERN
1652 HUGUENOT TRAIL
POWHATAN, VA 23139
PRIVATE RESIDENCE

POWHATAN CORRECTIONAL CENTER

Powhatan Correctional Center

In the late 1700s, Virginia employed both capital and corporal punishment to those who broke the mandated laws. Thomas Jefferson suggested building a "penitentiary" house to hold and reform criminals. After being ignored for over a decade, Benjamin Latrobe set to work on designing the first jail in Virginia. It was located west of Richmond and looked out over the James River, which flowed past it. The first prisoners were sent there in 1800, before the facility was fully completed in 1804. Virginia currently has fifty such institutions throughout the state (Virginia Department of Corrections 2016a).

The Powhatan Correctional Center is one of the oldest prison buildings existing today in the state. Built in 1926, the main structures of the facility were completed in 1952 and could hold up to 518 inmates at a time (McFarland 2014). They also allowed for different vocational work for some of the inmates, ranging from working in the milk plant, printshop, tag shop, and silkscreen shop (Virginia Department of Corrections 2016b).

A couple of stories surround the correctional center, which closed in 2015. One concerns the inmate infirmary, containing three windows, which are watched by staff in the security towers outside them. There have often been reports of a man looking out one of the windows. When they send someone to see who the person is and why he is on the property, no one is ever found. This is a secured area, and there is no way anybody could get in or out of the building without someone letting them through locked doors. One time, an officer reported seeing the man at the window, and the guard who went to investigate again stated that no one was present, but the officer could still see the gentleman standing there. He had no explanation for the man's appearance (Forgotten USA 2013).

Another time, it was an inmate who had a ghostly experience. He and his cellmate were retiring for the night when the event occurred. He was in the bottom bunk and just starting to drift off to sleep. He awoke to the feeling that someone else was in the cell with him and his cellmate. He knew it wasn't his cellmate, since he would have heard him climb down from the upper bunk. He also thought it was one of the guards checking on them, but then he realized he hadn't heard the loud clanging of the cell door opening.

He finally came to the conclusion that it was a spirit or demon of some kind. The entity leaned so close to the inmate that he could feel the body heat next to his head. A chanting of unknown words started, causing a low droning noise inside his head. His whole body froze, and he started having trouble breathing. Finally, after an interminable amount of time, he began to manage small movements at a time. After he gained control of his hands and arms, he finally leaped out of bed to confront the entity. There was no one in the cell except him and his cellmate (True Ghost Tales 2013).

POWHATAN CORRECTIONAL CENTER
3600 WOODS WAY
STATE FARM, VA 23160
804-598-4251
HTTPS://VADOC.VIRGINIA.GOV/FACILITIES/CENTRAL/POWHATAN/

SHILOH BAPTIST CHURCH

Shiloh Baptist was established in 1866 in the home of Doc Walton, according to the historical marker in front of the church. The congregation consisted of seventy ex-slaves who worshiped every Sunday. The first pastor's name was Daniel White. Their framed church burned down in 1898, and the current structure replaced it. The church has overcome many financial struggles, being demolished in 1884 in favor

Shiloh Baptist Church

of a brick building, and many different leaders to guide them through their scriptures (Shiloh Baptist Church 2016).

Inside the church is a beautiful mural painting completed in 1942 by Julien Binford, a local artist in Powhatan. The mural, located directly behind the pulpit in the archway, was also featured in the October 1942 issue of *Life* magazine. Since the congregation at the time could not afford to pay Binford, he took food and vegetables as his payment instead (McFarland 2016).

There is an older cemetery that sits behind the church, with many weathered stones that are unreadable or not engraved. There are also graves that are unmarked or only marked by a small stone. About two years ago, my dad and I were walking through just looking at the different stones when another person was visiting a loved one. We stopped and chatted with the woman for a few minutes, and she told us that some people had seen some misting at certain intervals, and a man in a black shirt and pants had been seen roaming the grounds. When approached, he would disappear into the trees behind the cemetery, never to be found. She told me the church encouraged a family-type atmosphere, and she would like to think these are friendly souls coming back to check on their loved ones.

SHILOH BAPTIST CHURCH
3198 MONTE ROAD
POWHATAN, VA 23139
804-598-5430
WWW.FACEBOOK.COM/PAGES/SHILOH-BAPTIST-
CHURCH/111766438859303

FINE CREEK BAPTIST CHURCH

Fine Creek Baptist Church

Small boy behind Martin headstone and in between two stones behind it

Located near the intersection of 711 and 522, this church has something for everyone. There is a beautiful sanctuary, a playground and picnic area in the back, and a well-kept cemetery. The church was founded back in the late 1700s, and Edward Maxey, the first pastor, started here in 1775. He remained pastor of the congregation until he died in 1781 of smallpox. The sanctuary that now stands on the property was constructed in 1903. Other additions were built over the years to facilitate the growth of the congregation, such as an educational building (1957), a parsonage (1961), a picnic pavilion (1985), and the fellowship hall (1993) (Fine Creek Baptist Church 2014).

I found this particular church by accident about two years ago when traveling down Route 711. Since I love to traipse cemeteries, I stopped to take a few pictures to see if I could capture anything. When the pictures came back, I was very surprised to find a small boy in one of them. I had been pulled to this particular spot, so I'd started taking pictures around it. Afterward, I'd walked a little more into the cemetery to find two small children's graves. It looked like a brother and a sister who had passed away in infancy. It was strangely eerie, since I didn't know if this little one was one of them, but it was interesting to see nonetheless. There are also some apparitions around the swing set near the back of the church. I have gone back several times to explore and photograph this peaceful cemetery.

Lady in a cloak is walking behind the swings to the right.
The lady may be difficult to see, so look closely.

FINE CREEK BAPTIST CHURCH
3619 HUGUENOT TRAIL
POWHATAN, VA 23139
804-403-3070
WWW.FINECREEKBAPTIST.ORG

BELNEMUS PLANTATION

Located near US Route 60, Belnemus is listed as a historic home on the county register. The Mayo family built the original part of the home in 1760. It is a two-story house with four pillars on the front and wings on both sides. A dairy shed and an equipment shed are among the other structures on the land.

Three mills worked hard at grinding corn during the Civil War for the Confederate army. There was also a smokehouse on the property that contained bacon and sides of ham for curing. Along with these buildings, there were slave quarters located behind the home (Taylor 1992).

After 1900, the plantation was for sale after the Scott family, who had previously owned the property, died. Burr Mayo and his wife, Lucy, came to see the charming home. They found a huge sofa and a cloudy mirror left behind. In the attic, two portraits were discovered, both unframed. One was of a very lovely girl, and the other was a male who was believed to have been cruel in life. Mayo glanced at them and returned them to their spot in the attic. He soon forgot about them with all the excitement about the house happening.

Mayo was sleeping on the couch one night around 2:00 a.m. when he awoke to a cold sensation. He stated that it felt like something cold touched his hand. He heard something move to the far end of the room. He was bewildered, since he had locked the door before going to bed and had blown out the candles. He said it was somebody walking, although it was an irregular rhythm. The sound of walking came up beside the bed, then turned around and went back down again. After the walking continued for a bit, the entity walked over to the sofa in the room and fell down upon it. The sofa creaked and groaned at the weight. Mayo finally got up and lit a candle to see who was playing tricks on him this late at night. After he lit the candle, he looked over toward the sofa and got a huge fright—no one was there (Taylor 1992).

After speaking with one of the former slaves, who was well past ninety, Mayo decided that the entity could possibly be Wild Jim Scott. Jim committed suicide in the house by cutting his throat or shooting himself in the head. Mayo also decided to rid himself of the sofa that sat in his room. As it was being carted up to the attic, Mayo noticed a large stain on one end of the sofa. He thought it could be the bloodstain from when Jim killed himself.

Later in the week, Lucy and a friend were up in the attic looking for something when they found the two old and dusty portraits again. The girl's image attracted Lucy, who thought there was something very familiar about her. She said the picture of the man had the most evil eyes she had ever seen. She decided to speak to the older ex-slave, like her husband had, to see if she could find out who was in the pictures (Taylor 1992).

She was not ready for the reaction she got from the old former slave. He was mad with rage, and she thought he was going to become violent. When she decided to go back once he calmed down, Mayo forbade her because it could be dangerous.

As Mayo walked along the garden fence one night, he saw Lucy sneak toward the old ex-slave's house. He could not fathom that she would directly disobey him. All he saw was a white shawl against the darkness; he never saw her face. He watched her until she arrived at the gate to the former slave's house. He then watched who he thought was Lucy pass right through the closed gate. He was quite taken aback at the sight.

He hurried back home to find Lucy dressed in a red dress and sewing some clothes back together. When he asked her about the garden incident, she swore she had not left the house (Taylor 1992).

Mayo finally decided the paintings needed to be moved farther back into the hole in the attic so they would cause no more trouble. Lucy joined him to watch, and all of a sudden she screamed and fell. Mayo lifted her to her feet and she asked why he pulled her over so roughly. He stated he hadn't been within ten feet of where she was standing. She said she could feel cold hands around her neck pulling her backward.

Mayo had had enough. He took the sofa with the bloodstain outside the next day and burned it completely. A violent storm occurred that night, with much lightning to add to the ominous roar. As he was standing in front of the fireplace, he turned around to see a sobbing woman who moved toward the door. As she approached it, she never reached for the doorknob; she just passed right through it. Mayo and Lucy ran toward the attic to find the portraits of the two people. When he saw the image of the young woman, he told Lucy about seeing her in front of the fireplace downstairs (Taylor 1992).

When morning came, Mayo hurried down to the former slave's quarters to ask the old man what was happening in the house. He was shocked to learn that the old slave had died during the storm the night before after being struck by a thunderbolt, according to the other slaves.

After much deliberation, Mayo deduced that Wild Jim had first killed the woman, then killed himself after he disposed of her body. Mayo burned the paintings plus everything the old slave had owned. The hauntings ceased after that.

Many months later, Mayo decided to build a new dwelling where the old ex-slave's quarters had stood. They started to dig around to seat a good foundation and came across a human skeleton maybe four feet deep in the dirt. She had been buried with no casket, and it seemed whoever did it was in a hurry at the time. They also found a tortoiseshell comb that Lucy's grandmother was known to wear (Taylor 1992).

Could the lady have been her grandmother? No one is certain of the identity of the buried woman. One hopes that she is now at peace, and that Wild Jim has followed. There are no reports of hauntings at this time; however, the story about Burr Mayo and his wife really brings it to life. It illustrates how a violent death may cause a spirit to linger until the important piece of information is found, releasing them from the earthly plane.

BELNEMUS PLANTATION
4950 ANDERSON HIGHWAY
POWHATAN, VA 23139
PRIVATE RESIDENCE
THE BELNEMUS PLANTATION IS ALSO KNOWN AS BELLE-NEMUS,
BELLNEMUS, AND BELLENMUS.

AMELIA

AMELIA WILDLIFE MANAGEMENT RESERVE

Amelia Wildlife Reserve is a 2,200-acre habitat open year-round for those who enjoy outdoor activities such as hunting, fishing, shooting ranges, and hiking along nature trails. It used be mostly farmland, but it is now a wildlife habitat. The park is surrounded on the north and east sides by the Appomattox River.

For hunters, there are squirrels, rabbits, quail, waterfowl, deer, and turkeys. The gun range has six different stations with targets ranging from twenty-five to one hundred yards. Shooters can practice with rifles, but no handguns are allowed. Fishing is available along the one-hundred-acre lake, and there are many varieties of fish available, such as crappie, catfish, largemouth and striped bass, and sunfish (Virginia Department of Game and Inland Fisheries 2016).

There are many ghost stories that are related to the wildlife reserve area. A charred lady roams the park along with several other apparitions (Haunted Places 2016e). There have also been reports that it is a popular spot for dumping murder victims. One of these victims was found near the entrance of the reserve, and the case was never solved. The other victim was located near the dam area, where a ghostly woman was spotted dragging a body. Is it the same person who was killed? Unfortunately, no one has identified the apparitions in the sightings (Kinney 2009).

When my brother and I visited the reserve, it was a clear, sunny day. There is a fork in the road when you first enter the reserve. The road on the right leads to the open wildlife area, and the road on the left leads to the shooting ranges. We parked by the wildlife reserve and decided to walk the rest of the way into the park since the gate was down. We walked a half mile down a dirt road, surrounded by trees on one side and foliage on the other, along with some wildflowers and vegetation. We both took a few pictures and departed. It is a great way to spend an afternoon just looking for animals, taking pictures, or looking for a ghost that may appear in the trees.

AMELIA WILDLIFE MANAGEMENT RESERVE
KENNONS LANE NEAR THE AMELIA COURTHOUSE BETWEEN ROUTES 60 AND 360
804-367-1000 (DEPARTMENT OF GAME & INLAND FISHERIES)
WWW.DGIF.VIRGINIA.GOV/WMA/AMELIA
MUST HAVE A LICENSE FOR ALL ACTIVITIES, INCLUDING HIKING. CLOSED ON MONDAYS.

HAW BRANCH PLANTATION

The Haw Branch Plantation, first settled by Colonel Thomas Tabb, is located near the Amelia Courthouse. The mansion on the property was built in 1745 and named for the trees that were growing down by the stream (Haunted Stories 2013, Virginia Haunted Houses 2016).

When the McConnaughey family purchased the plantation in 1965, they set about renovating it. As they upgraded their new home, peculiar things began to occur.

On a cold night in November 1965, the owners (William and Gibson) heard a horrible scream from the second floor of the mansion. They hurried through the upstairs rooms to come up empty-handed as to where the scream originated (Haunted Stories 2013).

Six months later, in May 1966, they heard several screams and found no one who could have caused the noise. This kept happening every six months in November and May until May 1968, when something changed. There were no screams, but they did hear the sound of someone walking across their front yard with very heavy shoes. There was a loud wail heard as well. On further investigation, they found it may have been a large bird. As of today, it is said that the sounds have ceased (Haunted Stories 2013).

Another story about the mansion concerns a portrait of a young woman named Florence Wright, who was related to the McConnaugheys by marriage. She died at twenty-four before the painting was completed. She had a massive stroke and was found lying across her piano. The artist of the portrait, J. Wells Champney, also died soon after Florence. He was in New York and accidentally fell down an elevator shaft (Taylor 2009).

The painting was then stored for twenty years in the upstairs of the mansion. The coloring in the painting was lighter pastels. When the painting was finally brought back down by Mrs. McConnaughey, all the colors had faded, and most had turned to a grayish hue. She decided to place the portrait in the library, where all could enjoy it. After a short time, voices began to be heard in the library that no one could explain. The painting itself started to return to its former glory. A medium stated that Florence was finally happy with the spot where the painting was located, so she restored its color (Virginia Haunted Houses 2016).

There are several other instances where the owners have found things happening with no logical explanation. Harriet Mason, great-grandmother to the family, is said to haunt the plantation. There are also three men who haunt the grounds. One hangs out in the barn, one cries for help and wears riding boots, and the third man walks with a limp and is described as very skinny (Haunted Places 2016f). The man in the barn brings a lantern with him as he walks through the barn's doorway. He will vanish if approached, but the lantern is left behind, hanging in midair (Hauck 2002).

There are also reports of happenings in the parlor of the mansion. There is a young woman in a portrait that is said to blush whenever you look at her for too long. Oftentimes, the parlor is filled with the sounds of people laughing and talking during parties, yet no one is ever seen (Shadowlands Haunted Places Index 1998). Additionally, there is a scent of citrus and roses throughout several rooms of the mansion (Hauck 2002).

With Florence happy about the location of her portrait, the color stays a beautiful hue, and she even blushes if you look long enough. What of the other spirits outside? Are they still roaming the property? Perhaps you will hear them crying for help or carrying a lantern so they can see how to get to their next destination.

HAW BRANCH PLANTATION
14017 HAW BRANCH LANE
AMELIA, VA 23002
PRIVATE RESIDENCE

AMELIA COURTHOUSE

Amelia Courthouse

Amelia Courthouse has a rich history starting decades before the Civil War. The county, established in 1849, was named after a daughter of King George II of Great Britain, Amelia Sophia. Robert E. Lee spent several days here in April 1865 waiting for supplies to arrive from Richmond, which never came. He asked that local people donate foodstuffs for his troops, everything from flour to vegetables and meat. He then continued onto Saylor's Creek and the battle that was to ensue at that location (American Courthouses 2013).

The courthouse was built in 1850 in colonial-style architecture. The front has four huge columns supporting the portico above. The old jail is to the left, near the road. Standing in front of the courthouse is a memorial statue to the Confederates who died in the Civil War. There is also a cannon from Lamkin's Battery, which stopped the advancement of the Union army. Four mortars were taken, and one blew up when used to salute the remains of Jefferson Davis (stated on cannon's plaque).

As for ghostly happenings, a gentleman told me this story the day that my brother and I were shooting pictures of the location. A dark figure walks in front of the courthouse at different intervals. When someone tries to approach it, the figure vanishes. It is thought to be a man, but no one is sure because its face is never seen.

AMELIA COURTHOUSE
16441 COURT STREET
AMELIA, VA 23002
804-561-2128
WWW.AMELIACOVA.COM/YOUR_GOVERNMENT/CIRCUIT_COURT.PHP

TRIBBLE FARM

As you drive down the street and up the driveway of this quaint family home, you imagine a bustling farm at work in the backyard. There are chickens and guineas all over, plus a mix of dogs, cats, and a few cows. I had met previously with the owners to discuss the happenings at the farm and arrange a good time to tour the house and barn. We met in Blackstone for a nice dinner and talked about the farm at length. It does have its own unique charm.

As you enter the back porch area, there is a white screened-in porch with a door. It is this door that will open, hang for a second, and then close as if someone has walked through the door to enter the house. The owners say it happens almost every night around 7:00 o'clock. They think it is one of the previous owners, Vernon, who used to milk his cows in the barn. He would take his boots off before entering the house to retire for the night.

The owners also note that the field between their house and the church down the road has an unusual occurrence. They would see a light, almost like a lantern, coming across the field at dusk. They always saw the light, but they never saw anyone carrying it. Once it traveled about halfway across the field, the light would disappear. They have not found out what is causing it.

After some research, the owners discovered that a soldier's body had been exhumed in the 1940s near where they see the light in the field. There is a story of a soldier around the same timeline who had just arrived at Fort Pickett. His ride had left him, so he found a ride with two other soldiers. Around 2:00 o'clock the next morning, they dropped the soldier near their house and told him he would have to walk the rest of the way, since they weren't going any farther. After a while,

Back door that opens and
closes by itself some nights

the soldier couldn't get a ride because it was so late. He walked back to the house where the two soldiers lived and knocked on the door. The father of the men was so mean that the entire family was scared to death of him. After the soldier knocked, the father told him to get off the property or he would shoot him. He knocked on the door again, and the father shot him through the door with buckshot, killing him. The two men buried him on the property. The father died in the 1960s, and his family finally told what had happened that night.

Upon walking through the back door, you come across a small hallway that leads into the kitchen. There have been many flashes of light and movement through this passageway. I started to feel cold, and I was pulled toward the kitchen very strongly.

In the kitchen, there is a wall that runs perpendicular to the hallway, where two baskets used to hang with food in them. The owner said she took them down because they were way-too-much fun for the ghosts. At Thanksgiving dinner, one of the baskets began to take on a life of its own, starting to swing back and forth like someone was pushing it, whereas the other remained absolutely still. After dinner, the swinging basket abruptly stopped as if it was halted in midair. The kitchen also had flashes of light and movement through it.

Taking pictures of every angle, we moved into the living room. As I moved through the living room, I was again very strongly pulled back toward the kitchen. I decided to stay and finish investigating the living room first.

There are several stories that surround the living room. The owner's mother spent several nights sleeping (or maybe not sleeping) on the couch. She stated she was kept awake all night by someone walking back and forth across the floor. She never saw anyone enter or leave the living room.

Also in the living room, there is a copy of the US Constitution hanging on the front wall. The owner, after snapping some pictures, noticed the face of a Confederate soldier in the bottom corner of the frame.

From the living room, you can make your way into the owner's bedroom, which has its own bathroom attached. She had thrown her robe across the tub one night and then remembered something she needed to retrieve from the kitchen. Upon returning to the bedroom, the robe had been neatly laid out on the bed like someone was wearing it. No one else was in the house at the time.

Her cats are also known to chase "things" on the wall at the head of her bed. They say several times it was lights from cars going down the street. Other times, there are no cars or lights, but the cats will still jump up on the bed to chase, scratch, and jump at the wall as if there is something there.

Perhaps the cutest story involving the owner's bedroom concerns a little boy she thinks is between seven and ten years of age. Her sister resides in the next room, and there is a connecting hallway between the two rooms that has now been closed off. When it was open, they would catch sight of the little boy peeking through into the owner's bedroom. Since the door has been shut, they have not seen him.

Heading back into the living room, there is an old bookcase with an antique clock on it. A friend of the family had stopped by to visit and was standing near the bookcase. She kept saying she heard voices coming from somewhere. Afterward, the friend ran out of the house, and she vowed never to return inside. As I stood there, all I heard was the sound of running water. The owner stated there was no water running anywhere in the house.

After that, we moved back to the kitchen, where I had gotten a very strong pull. I followed it to a door that was closed. I told the owner that the feeling was very strong in the particular spot, and asked what was behind the closed door. It led into her dining room. She began to move the table to show me why the room was giving off such a strong emanation. She had recently pulled up the carpet in this room and discovered a unique stain on the left side of the floor. The stain resembled a body lying on the floor: you could make out the head, torso, and two legs. She said her research revealed that a man had bled to death in this room in that spot.

Bloodstains forming a man's image on the dining-room floor

There is a bathroom attached to the dining area. The owner's daughter had a hair-raising experience in the room. She was what they called a "Ghost Virgin." She didn't believe in spirits nor had she ever seen one. She went in the bathroom and closed the door. A few minutes later, she came running out scared of something. The owner asked what had happened. The girl replied that while sitting, an orb of light came out of the shower curtain and stopped right in front of her face. It left by way of going through the bathroom door that was still closed. She stated that she was now a true believer.

We decided to move upstairs, since the doorway was at the other end of the dining room. The owner has taken a number of photographs of the steep

Steps where I was pushed backward, and many orbs are seen.

staircase. In one, a woman in Victorian garb is seen at the top.

As we ascended, I got a strong push at about the third step from the top. It was like someone had their hand on my chest and was pushing me backward. It was so intense; I simply asked the entity to please stop. The pressure lightened up a little, but you could still feel it very strongly. The attic has been the location for many orb sightings. The owner's son saw many of these while he was residing in the attic. If you blow up the orbs on a computer screen, you can see faces in some of them. If you are downstairs, you can hear many people walking around upstairs.

We made our way downstairs and started to peruse the outside of the home. The barn in the back held turkeys and chickens, which were relatively young. The big thing about the barn is that the chicken doors open by themselves every so often. Could it be Vernon still checking on his animals?

Behind the barn, an old family cemetery still keeps the secrets of the dead. It was overgrown and covered in foliage. There are foundation blocks to the right from a house that stood there years ago. To the left of the clearing, there is the cemetery near the bottom of the hill. They also have another cemetery near another house that belonged to a midwife. The front yard is full of graves of infants and mothers who died in childbirth from the 1800s, they think (Tribble and Tribble 2016).

TRIBBLE FARM
PRIVATE RESIDENCE

SAYLOR'S CREEK BATTLEFIELD

Encompassing four counties and containing 300 acres, this particular site has had many paranormal reports from people who come to record the sounds or simply take pictures of the battlefield itself. This battle took place almost seventy-two hours before Lee surrendered to Grant at Appomattox at the end of the Civil War (Tomlin 2010).

History records that over 2.5 million soldiers fought in the war both on the Confederate and Union sides. Out of these, between 600,000 and 800,000 men lost their lives during the battle (Godburn 2016). This gives a clear picture of the devastation caused on both sides, causing them to come to a surrender agreement on April 9, 1865.

Lee had already lost over 7,500 men, including his own son, George Washington Custis Lee. The date was April 6, 1865, known to historians as "Black Thursday." He had retreated from Richmond only to meet up with General Sheridan's company at this battlefield (Elton 2015).

The Confederate troops had been marching for almost four days toward Farmville, only to find their path blocked by the Union calvary. They had gone the previous two days without anything to eat, and they were hoping to find something around the Amelia Courthouse area. There was nothing so they continued into the Saylor's Creek area, where the Hillsman family handed them what food they could spare as the soldiers marched by the house (Taylor 2007).

The Hillsman House functioned as a hospital for the wounded both on the Confederate and Union sides. If you tour the house, make a note to stand and look outside the front door. The field across the road is where the second out of three battles fought in the area took place. The battle started near Hillsman House and spread out across the battlefield on both sides. The Battle of Sailor's Creek included three engagements known as Battle of Lockett's Farm, Battle of Hillsman's Farm, and Battle of Marshall's Crossroads (Elton 2015). Lockett's Farm still has numerous bullet holes in the house's frame. Marshall's Crossroads brought both cavalries together for a major battle (Sailor's Creek Battlefield Historical State Park n.d.).

After this great battle at Sailor's Creek, both Grant and Lee knew the fighting was coming to an end. After Black Thursday, the morning of April 7, 1865, brought the starting of a dialogue between Grant and Lee. Two days later, Lee surrendered

Saylor's Creek Battlefield, and off in the distance, you can see Hillsman House.

to grant at the Appomattox Courthouse after losing a total of 8,800 men, including several generals (Civil War Trust 2014c).

The aftermath was described by a Union cavalryman in a very poetic way. He had written in his diary about the dead lying strewn across the battlefield, almost like leaves on the ground in autumn. Many soldiers who were walking across the fields had to tread carefully so as not to step on the dead soldiers (Calkins 2015). Many of them lay in the fields for up to three weeks. The soldiers who were not claimed by their families were either buried where they lay or placed in a mass grave in the fields or down by the streams. The quiet of the battlefield became deathly eerie after that.

Near the visitor center, there is an overlook where you can see the Hillsman House on the next hill. It was a beautiful scene, making me pause as I stood there trying to absorb what had happened 150 years ago on this very spot. I thought about the bloody battle that had occurred here, and wondered how the men survived and dealt with their everyday marching and fighting. I cannot imagine the horrors or the pain they all endured.

I made my way down the Confederate Outlook Trail and headed toward the creek at the bottom of the hill. The trail is well marked, and you will cross two wooden bridges along the way. I recorded my journey down the hill, and before I arrived at one of the bridges, there was a sound heard on the recorder for about five seconds. It was like someone had blown into it. I did hear the wind; however, that was more of a high-pitched sound. This came out as a very low, breathy sound, almost as if someone were saying "Ahhhhh!"

I made my way to the creek bed, which was considerably dry. You could look up the hill and see the back of the Hillsman House. There were two benches and another path at the other end of the creek bed that led back up the hill. The creek and ravine were where the dead soldiers were buried. They would gather the bodies and place them in the ravine, covering them with dirt. None of these graves are marked, and it is the hope of the Saylor's Creek Society to do some underground detecting to see if they can find some of the sites where this may have occurred (Godburn 2016).

As I started back up the hill, I chose to follow the path around the other side of the hill. It would take me back to my original trail, and I would see the whole area. When I made it about halfway up the hill, I started to get the feeling that someone was watching me. In fact, every few minutes, I would turn around and look back to see if someone was there. I was alone on the trail. After ten minutes, I got a weird feeling, and I looked again behind me. This time, it felt like someone was following me back up the hill. I could hear someone walking on the trail behind me. I could make out the footsteps along with the leaves rustling and the crunch on the rocks. When I turned around to check, no one was there. For the rest of my ascent up the hill, I kept feeling like someone was behind me. It was not a malevolent feeling, just a curious one. Right after this, I started to hear tapping noises for about twenty seconds on my recorder. I thought at first that it might be a woodpecker; however, the noise was too loud for a bird in the distance to be making.

As I walked back up the path,
I turned back several times as I
heard someone following me.
I also had the feeling of being
watched several times.

Visitor Center tree where
two men met the same
apparition a year apart

I finally made it back to the top and headed back to the visitor center. My tour guide, Jim, had told me there was an occurrence at one of the cedar trees beyond the picnic area. Two men had the same experience a year apart. They both were reenacting a scene from the battle and made a campsite for the night. They were asleep with their fire burning down. All of sudden, they woke up with the feeling that someone was crouched and looking over them. One of the men said something actually tapped his foot a couple of times (Godburn 2016).

There are other stories from the battlefield of ghostly apparitions. There is a narrow bridge down from the Hillsman House, going toward the visitor center. The fog apparently gets very heavy in this area, sometimes giving people chills. Some have said they have seen soldiers walking down the road in this area as well.

Are there spirits from long ago hanging around the battlefield, waiting for the raging war to be over? We can only hope they win the day and have plenty of food to enjoy.

Note: I wanted to include a short endnote about the name of the battlefield. You will see it as Sailor's Creek, Sayler's Creek, or Saylor's Creek. The spelling depends on who is writing the piece. The earliest maps of the battle had Sailor's Creek. The name for the creek that runs down beside where the battle was fought was named Sayler's Creek. There is a discrepancy, but the Civil War Sites Advisory Commission stated that Sailor's Creek would be the proper spelling of the battle and location. That is not to say everyone follows the rule, but there is a ruling on which name is correct (Civil War Trust 2014c).

SAYLOR'S CREEK BATTLEFIELD
6541 SAYLER'S CREEK ROAD
RICE, VA 23966
804-561-7510
WWW.DCR.VIRGINIA.GOV/STATE-PARKS/SAILORS-CREEK#GENERAL_
INFORMATION
HOURS: MONDAY–SATURDAY, 10:00 A.M. TO 5:00 P.M.; SUNDAY, 12:00 P.M.
TO 5:00 P.M.
SELF-GUIDED TOURS AND TOURS BY APPOINTMENT ARE OFFERED.

HILLSMAN HOUSE

Front of Hillsman House

Located on a 1,500-acre farm, the 1½-story house built by Moses Overton was completed in 1780. In 1815, the addition of a full basement was used as a kitchen. It also had a brick foundation and clapboard walls. One of the younger daughters, Martha, married John Hillsman. The dwelling became known as the Overton-

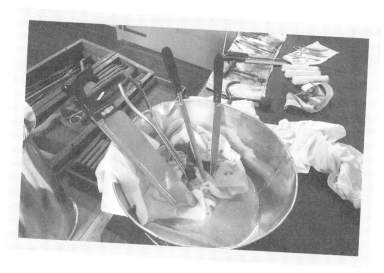

Surgical instruments used during the Civil War for an amputation

Hillsman House and served as a family home until the war came across the fields in front of the home.

When the soldiers came, they locked the family living in the house down in the cellar for the four days they were in residence to keep them out of harm's way. Both Confederate and Union soldiers were treated at this makeshift hospital for only three to four days during the war. At least 500 wounded men were brought here to have surgery or to set their broken bones. Out of the 500, there were 161 Confederate soldiers and 339 Union soldiers. The wounded soldiers were placed inside the house, and everyone else who was not in critical condition lay on pallets on the ground outside the house. Even after the surrender agreement was made at Appomattox, there were still many surgeons from both sides still working on the wounded men (Godburn 2016).

Our tour guide for the house, Jim, reminded us of several things we have today that doctors didn't have during the war. These included no blood transfusions, no IVs for hydrating a patient, and no anesthesia to use for a local, such as when setting a broken finger or arm. They used ether or chloroform for amputations or trying to get bullets and shrapnel out of an abdomen.

Being an operating-room nurse myself, I was fascinated with the instruments and other procedures that he explained to us. The instrumentation looked almost the same as it does today. It had just changed from a wooden handle on the amputation saw to a stainless steel handle, since you can't sterilize wood.

Another interesting thing to note was they had no sterility at all and no concept of a sterile environment. The table used for surgeries was often covered in the last patient's blood when the next man was placed on it. Surgeons and their assistants did not wash their hands between procedures either. Another factor in keeping wounds clean was the location's access to clean water. Dug in the eighteenth or nineteenth centuries, the well was only about twenty-five feet deep and caught mostly groundwater, which was muddy. Animals such as horses and mules traveled up and down the road and could drop hundreds of pounds of feces that got washed into the system as well. In turn, the surgeons and others used this water to clean wounds, drink, wash dishes, and cook (Godburn 2016).

As mentioned earlier, over 2.5 million men (Confederate and Union) served during the war. Out of those, 600,000–800,000 died. Two out of every three men died of a disease not related to their wounds, such as dysentery, pneumonia, and typhoid (Godburn 2016). Just think what an antibiotic could have done back then for all these health issues.

The tour started with a short history outside the house, and learning about the extent of the war in the area. Two other homes, Lockett Farm and Harper House, also served as hospitals for the wounded in the area. However, the battle that took place at Saylor's Creek was by far the bloodiest and most violent. Jim went onto explain some of the history before the war. The Hillsman family members were farmers who had many major crops such as corn, wheat, and vegetables, along with some peach and apple trees. The major crop was tobacco.

The house has stayed in remarkable shape since 1865, since there have always been people living in it and keeping the repairs current. A full restoration was completed less than ten years ago. There is still family both for the Hillsmans and the Overtons in the area. They help upkeep the cemetery on the property and the home, and several also sit on the board of the Saylor's Creek Battlefield Organization (Godburn 2016).

Upon entering the house, there are two big wooden doors on the back of the house. This was to help keep drafts out in the winter. As you enter the doorway, you notice the "old-house" smell. It is an earthy, musty type of scent. I began to feel chills when I stepped through the door, but nothing outstanding.

The first room you step into is made to look like a working surgery setup of the time, with a table, amputation instruments set out, and plenty of bloody gauze everywhere. There was even a carrying stretcher and a medical pannier, which held all the drugs they would have used. According to some eyewitness reports, twenty to thirty surgeons and their assistants worked twenty-four hours a day on the wounded. Having taken the Hippocratic oath, they worked both on Union and Confederate soldiers. There are also bloodstains all over the floor, which are covered in Plexiglas so that they can be further tested (Godburn 2016).

As you move into the second room, you see how it could have been a "great room" for both families, almost like a living room today. Today, you will notice two beds in the nearest corners. There is also room for pallets for other soldiers to rest. The first soldier ever brought here was George Peck. He was wounded down by the creek near the house. He wrote about all his experiences while treated as a patient there. Because of his notes, we can surmise what the battle was like and what the men went through during their time at the hospital. His head was by the door so he could watch the surgeons working all night long to save the wounded. The two beds were for the severely wounded, and there were usually around six others in distress as well. Many men died in this room from their injuries (Godburn 2016).

On top of the fireplace in this room is a painting of James Moses Hillsman. He started out as a farmer until the war broke out in the area. He then joined the 44th Confederate Army to serve in the war effort. He quickly moved from sergeant to captain within three years. He was wounded three times during the war and was finally captured at the battle of Spotsylvania Courthouse in May 1864. He remained a prisoner of war for the rest of the war, and he was released in 1865 to return home.

The third room of the house is part of the addition to the home. It was completed in 1815 and included an attic room above it. It was a quiet room where the women could sew, knit, or read; the men could take care of their business affairs. This room has a wall that faces northeast, so the walls are made from plaster and lath. It served to keep the walls insulated during the cold winter months. After this, we headed down to the cellar (Godburn 2016).

The steps going down to the cellar are very steep and narrow. In fact, you have to go down sideways because you can't fit your whole foot on the step. It is amazing, once you get down the steps, to turn around and look back at what you just walked down. The cellar was used as a kitchen area, and they had the fireplace going twenty-four hours a day. There were many tasks to be accomplished each day, such as meal preparation, washing dishes and laundry, and rendering of fat for soap and candles. The heat would drift upward through the house, which was nice in the winter but not so inviting in the summer. (Remember the family that was locked down here during the war? It would have been in the beginning of April 1865, so it may not have been too hot for them. They had food to eat as well, so they were doing fine.)

The cellar was the first section of the house to be done, having been dug out by enslaved workers. The cellar is roughly 3½ feet underground, and it does have windows that look out onto the property. The foundation that you see is the original bricks surrounding the fireplace and chimney. Some of the wood beams in the ceiling have been replaced, and you can tell which ones if you look at them. The new beams were placed during the restoration, and they have saw marks on them. The older ash beams are from the 1700s and have rough cuts on them from the saw mill. The most impressive beam is by the fireplace. It is a 12-by-12-foot solid piece of wood (Godburn 2016). I can't imagine how they got it in there, let alone how they held it up to get it fixed in place.

That concluded the tour of the house. Everyone left, and I stayed behind to ask Jim some questions about happenings and about seeing the cemetery. We walked back upstairs, and he offered to let me go upstairs to take some pictures. It was mainly some storage rooms up there, one on either side. I took pictures and came back down to wait for Jim to lock up the house.

Before we left, I asked if there were any interesting stories about the house he could tell me. He mentioned that some visitors had seen a little boy, roughly five years old, running back and forth across the great room, where the soldiers had been placed to rest after surgery. He also said there was a male presence upstairs that was apparently felt as malevolent by some people. I got a twinge as I ascended

159

Great Room; a little boy is sometimes seen running through the corridor.

the stairs, but I did not get the impression of anything mean or unsettling. Jim told me about a lady who went upstairs and said she needed to go outside for a minute. He thought maybe she needed some air or had to answer a call on her phone. He walked down to check on her, and she was outside wiping her arms and torso down. She explained that she was a Reiki practitioner and felt the negativity in the attic. She was trying to wipe it off any way she could. (Being a Reiki III practitioner myself, this is how we "wipe" negative energy off people.)

We stepped outside, and Jim told me about other structures that would have sat on the grounds back then. There would have been the slave quarters, barns, a bathhouse, an icehouse, a smokehouse, and a carpenter's shed. He said probably six or more in total. The historical society is hoping to do some ground-penetrating radar to see if they can locate the foundations of the structures that once sat around the Hillsman house. As we walked back toward the parking lot to head to the cemetery, Jim pointed out another well that may have been around since the twentieth century. He stated the household might very well have had a rudimentary indoor plumbing system.

We made our way across the parking lot toward the picnic area. There is a path that leads down to the cemetery here. The path is not really visible, and you should take care in walking back there, especially in the summer months. There is an enclosure that has three graves of the Hillsman family. Over to the left of the enclosure is the grave for Moses Overton, who has a service marker from the War of 1812. Down below the family graves is a wooded area that spreads out back to the road. In the winter, you can see depressions in the ground across the field; however, it isn't known if they were slave or soldier graves (Godburn 2016).

The soldiers who died on the field were buried where they lay, and some were buried in mass graves. Some of the bodies lay exposed for up to three weeks before they were buried in mass graves around the property. There could be many soldiers under your feet as you walk these battlefields (Kinney 2012). Some of these soldiers were disinterred within one year and placed in Poplar Grove Cemetery in Petersburg. The families who retrieved the bodies would take them to their own family plots. There are 4,000 graves at Poplar Grove that are unmarked today. Roughly fifty are identified Union soldiers, and their place of death is marked as Saylor's Creek (Godburn 2016).

Some of the most haunted sections of the battlefield are at the Hillsman House, the Hillsman Cemetery, and the creek down by the cemetery. There have been many times a visitor has spotted a man in a blue uniform walking the property, only to find out later that there were no people dressed up in Civil War uniform that day. People have also heard voices in the house and in the woods behind the house. They have also heard proof that the battle continues on in a time long past. It is said if you stand very still and listen very closely, you can hear the cannon fire and the screaming of the men who fought the war so long ago (Kinney 2012). On one of the back hills of the house, people have seen a soldier and his horse standing—waiting for the battle to end (Godburn 2016).

HILLSMAN HOUSE
6541 SAYLER'S CREEK ROAD
RICE, VA 23966
804-561-7510
WWW.VIRGINIA.ORG/LISTINGS/MUSEUMS/HILLSMANHOUSE/
TOURS ARE FREE AND BY APPOINTMENT. ASK FOR JIM OR ZACHARY; THEY BOTH ARE VERY KNOWLEDGEABLE ABOUT THE BATTLE AND THE HOUSE.

CUMBERLAND/NELSON

CUMBERLAND

Charles Irving Thornton gravestone

BEAR CREEK LAKE STATE PARK

Bear Creek Lake State Park offers many welcoming amenities for their guests. They appeal to the people who really love the outdoors. Some of the activities you can enjoy are swimming, fishing (saltwater and trout), and camping. Pets are welcome as long as they are on a leash. They also offer eleven hiking trails ranging from easy to difficult (Bear Creek Lake State Park n.d.).

The 320-acre park was founded in 1939. The area has had its share of famous visitors, such as Charles Dickens, George Washington, Thomas Jefferson, and Patrick Henry. It was given its current name in 1958 after campgrounds were added (Elton 2015).

As you travel into the park, you will come across a historical marker just off the road for Jesse Thomas, a colonel who was wounded in the Revolutionary War; he was considered to be related to one of the First Families in Virginia. As the story goes, Jesse had been convalescing at home during the Revolutionary War. On June 2, 1781, he noticed a loud banging at his door. An escaped prisoner stood there amid the wind and rain coming down. The prisoner had come to warn him that British soldiers were headed toward his home. Jesse, even though he was quite ill, jumped on his horse, Fearnaught, and raced through the storm and even crossed the raging currents of a river on the way. He finally found Baron von Steuben and warned him that Cornwallis was on the way toward Steuben's current location.

Cabin 2

Famed author Charles Dickens also visited the lake, searching for the grave of Charles Thornton, who died at thirteen months of age. He wrote the child's epitaph for the gravestone, as requested by the child's doctor. This is only one of two epitaphs Dickens wrote in his lifetime, the other one being for his sister-in-law (Elton 2015). The gravesite is located down Oak Hill Forest Road in the Cumberland State Forest. It is back in a field nestled in a grove of trees and high grass. Some of Charles Thornton's other family members are also buried there.

Cabin 2 has been the subject of much discussion, since visitors continue to mention strange sounds and occurrences after staying in the cabin. Apparently, around 3:00 a.m., a rhythmic type of chopping sound is heard. Then there is a loud crack as the piece of wood splits into two parts. These sounds continue for a long time. When the people in the cabin arise the next morning, they go and look for pieces of wood all over the ground, only to find nothing there. Some seem to think it is Jesse Thomas's slave trying to keep his house warm and ready for battle. Others seem to think it is young Charles's father keeping the fire warm for his son.

There is a journal in the cabin that visitors write in, leaving a record of what happened to them on their visit. They started the journal in 2007, and it lists many other unusual occurrences within the cabin and on the grounds. These include faucets turning on by themselves, guests actually encountering a ghost and hearing it groan, and peanut butter jars being opened and left unclosed. There are also strange, scratchy noises heard coming from the windows and the walls. One bedroom hosts an apparition that sits on the bed. One visitor stated that the weight of someone sitting down on the bed was felt, but no one was there. There is also a walking stick that mysteriously shows up on the front porch of the cabin on different days (Elton 2015).

BEAR CREEK LAKE STATE PARK
22 BEAR CREEK LAKE ROAD
CUMBERLAND, VA 23040
804-492-4410
WWW.DCR.VIRGINIA.GOV/STATE-PARKS/BEAR-CREEK-LAKE#GENERAL_
INFORMATION

NELSON

MARK ADDY INN

Mark Addy Inn

The Mark Addy Inn is one of those places off the beaten path, but it still will give you welcome and cozy feelings despite its extra guests. There is a parlor where you can sit and read, plan your next adventure, or enjoy the twenty-three-year-old parrot, Baby, whose cage is against the back wall. The dining room is large enough for many people to sit comfortably, and they serve breakfast every morning (Tal 2016).

On the site where a log cabin once stood on the property, the Mark Addy Inn was completed in the 1800s, built by Charles Everett in the Wintergreen valley. Everett was also Thomas Jefferson's physician, and they spent many relaxing hours together. Everett had no children, but he took great pride in one of his nephews, John. John followed in Charles's footsteps and became a doctor (Mark Addy Inn 2016).

The one thing Charles did not like about John was the fact that he owned many slaves. He tried to make him see his error by leaving everything to John upon his death. If John didn't free the slaves, he would receive only one specific manor. John refused and inherited only Upland Farm. His son, John Coleman, married the first postmistress of Lodebar, which today is known as Nellysford, having been named after Nelly Martin, the woman John Coleman married.

Together, they built the current structure and added a room for every child of theirs—seven in total. There are many relatives of the family still living in and around Nelson County. Sometimes, visitors and guests are able to meet descendants of the family when they visit the inn to keep up with the daily happenings (Mark Addy Inn 2016).

John Maddox bought Upland Farm in the 1990s, and he found the need to rename it. Using his grandparents' names of Mark and Adalaide, the Mark Addy Inn was created. I spoke with John at length about the inn and some of the strange occurrences. He told me he never really felt anything except for the room at the top of the stairs off to the right. He always thought there was something in there, although he couldn't say exactly what it was (Maddox 2017). Currently, Leslie and Rafael Tal own the inn, which can serve as a great weekend getaway or a wonderful vacation spot (Mark Addy Inn 2016).

When my brother and I toured the inn, we were amazed at the beautiful surroundings and friendly staff. Jen, one of the staff, gave us a tour of the building and outside while we were there. The inn is painted in blue and yellow and has a gorgeous fountain out front. There is a cottage behind the inn where Jen lives at present, and it is known as the Innkeeper's Quarters. She told me a story about her dog getting loose one day, and her having to chase after him. There is a lamppost to the right of the inn, and just as she caught up with her dog, she noticed a woman standing under the post. She naturally thought it was a guest out for an evening stroll. Jen spoke and waved to the woman, but there was no response as the woman kept staring at her. She quickly decided to retreat into the house. The next morning, Jen asked some of the other residents and staff about the red-headed woman with shoulder-length hair. They all said they hadn't seen this person currently staying at the inn (Tal 2016).

As for haunting experiences, there are many to share. Some of the people we talked to who were staying at the inn stated they heard someone walking the halls at night. When they got up to see who it was after a while, no one was ever found.

Jen has seen a gentleman standing in the kitchen at certain times. She catches a glimpse of him and then he disappears. She is not sure who it is. Her mother-in-law, Leslie Tal, likes to take pictures both inside and outside the inn. She has taken many

Lamppost where a lady was staring at Jen

pictures of orbs throughout the home. When she watches the security cameras, she also states they have seen a glowing orb floating through the house and down the stairs. There is also a mirror on the stairs where orbs are seen with no reflection. Jen makes it clear that the energy around them is a good energy. There is no malevolence felt whatsoever (Tal 2016).

The owner, Leslie Tal, also says there is a problem with slanting pictures that will not hang correctly throughout the inn. She thinks it is Nelly Everett who is causing the slanting as well as the appearing orbs. These occur mostly in the Rue de Monet Room. The staff will straighten the pictures, and the next morning they all are slanted again. They have tried everything from new nails to moving the pictures to a different spot, but they will be crooked by the time someone enters the room (Koerting 2012).

There are two rooms where people have passed away. Since a doctor owned the inn at its beginnings, it only makes sense that people would come there for help if they needed it. There is a little girl who roams one room. The room was very heavy at first; it was redecorated and reorganized and is much lighter in energy now (Tal 2016). The owner thinks the young girl could be one of the Everett children, since one died at age fifteen from appendicitis (Koerting 2012). As I went from room to room, I found that the whole inn was very light in energy. There were no heavy feelings at all, giving credence to Jen's feeling that the energy at the inn is benevolent.

As I was taking the tour, I was pulled to a room at the top of the stairs, called the Colonel. It was a very strong presence that I felt all over the room. After taking many pictures, we had many iffy shots, but with the sunlight coming in the windows, we decided that they were sun refractions on the pictures (Tal 2016). (This is the room the original owner also thought was haunted.) The owner has stated that there

Staircase where orbs are seen

is a remarkable hotspot of energy on this staircase and toward the second floor (Koerting 2012).

We moved onto the Elena Room, where Jen explained that it had the creakiest floors in the inn. They sure enough did. This room has its own adjoining balcony, which connects to the original front porch on the side of the house (Tal 2016).

In the Mimosa Room, Jen told us about another of the staff who complained of an extra guest as well. A mischievous entity turns on the water faucet in the bathroom whenever someone is near the door. Whenever staff is cleaning, the faucet will continually turn on by itself even after they shut it off tight (Tal 2016).

In the Schloss Room, there is a light that turns on and off by itself. Guests will wake during the night to find it turned back on again. Some guests have even seen it turn on when they were doing outside activities (Koerting 2012). Of course, when the room is checked, no one is ever found near the light or in the room.

When the owner's daughter was married on the property, her brother took pictures during the ceremony. In one, an entity was found looking out of one of the inn's windows. They discovered that the next picture had no evidence of the entity (Koerting 2012).

Just a short note here about the animals at the inn. There is the chihuahua, a sweet little cat named Itty Bitty Kitty, a cat named Dahdilee, two black Pomeranians, and the previously mentioned twenty-three-year-old parrot named Baby, who resides in the parlor. The parrot can be very talkative at times, and he is a very beautiful fellow. You can enjoy nature while walking the grounds or hang out in the parlor reading and relaxing with the animals. This location has something for everyone.

MARK ADDY INN
56 RODES FARM DRIVE
NELLYSFORD, VA 22958
434-361-1101
WWW.MARK-ADDY.COM

SWANNANOA PALACE

Swannanoa Palace

This historic palace is located right near Afton Mountain, just off the Blue Ridge Parkway. Built by Major James Dooley in 1913, the surrounding property totaled 762 acres. The palace was to be a summer home for his wife to escape the humidity of Richmond. Traveling to Richmond, one will find the Maymont Estate, which is considered a cousin to the palace and is located near Byrd Park (Dulaney n.d.).

James Dooley was a very prolific man, having obtained a law degree from Georgetown University and enlisting in the Confederate army. He met his wife, Sallie May, in Staunton. After the war, he was elected mayor of Richmond and served in the state legislature. Passing away in 1922, he left much of his fortune and property to an orphanage and library. He also gave funds to build a much-needed medical facility in the area. Swannanoa Palace was left to Sallie May, who in turn left it to her husband's two sisters. It became the Swannanoa Country Club after the Valley Corporation bought it in 1926. Calvin Coolidge, US president at the time, stayed for a week playing golf and enjoying a Thanksgiving dinner. From 1949 to 1998, the University of Science and Philosophy held the lease to the sprawling property. Walter and Lao Russell lived there during this time.

It has changed hands many times since then. Currently, James and Sandy Dulaney own the mansion and are trying to raise funds to restore it to its previous splendor (Dulaney n.d.). They have plans to transform the fifty-two-room palace into a bed and breakfast and weekend getaway. At present, they offer tours of the palace, which is a great location for weddings. It has also had its share of famous visitors, including Ted Kennedy, Jackie Kennedy, Gerald Ford, Henry Kissinger, Queen Elizabeth II, and Margaret Thatcher (Taylor 1992).

At first glance, Swannanoa seems to be in ruins, but the Dulaneys are trying to have it refurbished. Sadly, the rooms are all bare, with just a few things left in the huge mansion to show what it used to be like. The fireplaces are extremely ornate, as are the ceilings. The staircase leading to the second floor is simply gorgeous. The stained-glass window at the top of the stairs has withstood the test of time and is stunning to behold, especially when the sun's light shines down through it (Virginia Beach Family Fun 2015). The stained-glass picture contains 4,000 pieces and shows Sallie herself in the back garden. As you wander through the palace, you will notice many likenesses of Sallie, such as on the first-floor ceiling, depicting her in a chariot. These tributes are all over the beautiful home (see Swannanoa Palace: Haunted and Mournful).

Inside and out, the building's design is a sight to see. Because it was built in Italian Renaissance style, there are many attributes you would not find in similar homes. It has Carrera marble on the interior of the home and Georgian marble on the exterior. Intriguingly, there is a lookout tower on the third floor, but be careful up here, since it can get very windy. The magnificent palace also boasts a dumbwaiter, an elevator, and a kitchen in the basement (Colchicine 2016). Taking almost three years to complete, the palace required the work of 300 artisans and workers. There are also many hidden doorways and passages all over the Palace (Swannanoa Palace: Haunted and Mournful).

The home was dubbed "Swannanoa" because of Sallie May's love of graceful white swans. If you look carefully upon entering the home, you will see a swan carved over the main door. There are also other swans hidden throughout the mansion. Some fixtures are made of gold, and the home contained the first electricity

Sallie in the stained glass window

169

in the area. They even had their own private power plant to keep the mansion well lit at all times (Colonial Ghosts 2016). The property has a garden gazebo and a family cemetery down the driveway when you walk out the front door. You can find Walter and Lao Russell buried there beside each other.

Many ghostly happenings have occurred within the walls of the palace. Sallie May herself is thought to be one of the entities; she is often seen roaming the corridors of the palace. Dulaney even states his cats will not go up past the third floor for some reason. There are also ghostly voices that many attribute to servants who worked in the domicile. The most active room in the palace is considered to be the library (Colonial Ghosts 2016). Twisted Paranormal Society did a session and captured many voices saying specific words and laughing. They also caught shadows blocking out certain things in the pictures. They caught footsteps coming down the stairway from the left tower. They also noticed that wherever they went in the house, most of them had the eerie sensation of being followed, but no one was ever seen behind them. Some of the best spots include the library, the two towers, the third floor, and on the grand stairway (Twisted Paranormal Society 2015b).

Lao Russell had many unexplained occurrences herself. One time she was very ill, and she told a story about a rainbow from the sky landing on the top of the palace. Once the rainbow touched the palace, Lao received immediate healing from the ailment she was suffering from at the time. Another time, she had what she called a vision from God. After Walter and Lao moved in, they discovered some bad pipes in the basement, which was going to cost around $50,000 to fix. She asked God's help in finding the leak, in hopes that they might repair it themselves. It cost only $85 to dig the problem area up, and Lao led them straight to the problem pipe after asking God to send her a vision as to where the issue was located. After much research into the history of the palace, they did find out that several Jesuit missionaries were killed on the property around 300 years ago by Indians in the area (Taylor 1992).

Another group of investigators found orbs in many pictures captured on the first floor of the palace. They thought it was a servant still trying to maintain the upkeep on the huge palace (Swannanoa Palace: Haunted and Mournful). It could also be Sallie May wondering why her beautiful home is in such disrepair. Could it also be Walter or Lao coming back to entice more followers of their studies? We may never know the answer.

SWANNANOA PALACE
497 Swannanoa Lane
Afton, VA 22920
540-945-5201
www.nelsoncounty-va.gov/Organization/swannanoa-palace/
Limited hours; call first. The trip would be good for a gorgeous ride over the mountain and heading toward Skyline Drive on a warm spring day.

CONCLUSION

Thank you for taking this fascinating journey with me. I hope you will plan to visit some of the locations mentioned in the book. As I stated, everything and everyone in Virginia seem to be all interconnected somehow. You may find people who are looking for the same thing you are.

Did you find the answer to the question that has plagued us all? What is beyond death?

Our loved ones are still with us, we just need to open our hearts and minds to see them. When you hear a spirit whistling, see a rocking chair moving even though no one is sitting in it, or feel a pinch going up the stairs, you may change your mind about that other world. Take a tour of a battlefield, a winery, or an old hospital from the Civil War, you may hear and see more than you thought possible. I know I have.

Despite the content of the book, I would like to state that none of it was written by a ghostwriter. *Mwha ha ha!*

BIBLIOGRAPHY

Abrams, Max, and Deon Abrams. Interview and tour with author (Grayhaven Winery), November 2016.

Albemarle County Historical Society. *Historic Charlottesville Tour Book.* Charlottesville, VA: Albemarle County Historical Society, 2002, www.jmrl.org/ebooks/Historic%20Charlottesville%20Tour%20Bo.pdf.

Albemarle County Old Jail Museum. "Reviving Albemarle's Historic Jail: Raising Awareness about the Jail's History and the Need to Preserve It." Last modified 2014, www.Oldjail.org/history.html.

American Courthouses. "Amelia County." Last modified 2013, www.courthouses.co/us-states/v-z/Virginia/Amelia-County.

Antique Properties. "Montebello." Last modified July 2009, www.antiqueproperties.com/3114.

Audibert, Phil. *All Four Years: A Civil War Driving Tour of Orange County, Virginia.* Orange, VA: Orange County Department of Tourism, 2011.

Baars, Samantha. "Local Haunt: Protected Farm Has Paranormal History." C-ville, January 2016, www.c-ville.com/local-haunt-protected-farm-paranormal-history/#.V8wk9JiU2M8.

Barefoot, Coy. "Then and Now: An Illustrated Journey through Time." *UVA Magazine*, October 2010, http://uvamagazine.org/articles/then_and_now1/.

BBOnline.com. "The Silver Thatch Inn." Last modified 2016, www.bbonline.com/united-states/Virginia/Charlottesville/silverthatch.html.

Bear Creek Lake State Park. *Trail Guide.* Cumberland, VA: Virginia State Parks, n.d.

Bearinger, David. "The Ghost of Belmead." Last modified March 2015, www.virginiahumanities.org/2015/03/the-ghost-of-belmead.

Blue Ridge Gazette. "Virginia's Haunted Places." Last modified October 2006, http://blueridgegazette.blogspot.com/2006/10/Virginias-haunted-places.html.

Blue Ridge Pottery. "Our Story." Last modified 2015, www.blueridgepottery.com/our-story.

Brandy Station Foundation. "Graffiti House." Last modified March 2017, www.brandystationfoundation.com.

Breeden, Martha. Interview and tour of Main Street with author (Madison County), November 2016.

Brown, Beth. *Haunted Plantations of Virginia.* Atglen, PA: Schiffer, 2009.

Cairns, Taylor. "Historic Mansion in Charlottesville Attracting Ghost Hunters after Viral Story." *Newsplex*, January 2016, www.newsplex.com/home/headlines/historic-mansion-in-charlottesville-attracting-ghost-hunters-after-viral-story-366789681.html.

Calkins, Chris. "From Sailor's Creek to Cumberland Church: Seventy-Two Hours before Appomattox," *Blue & Grey: For Those Who Still Hear the Guns* 31, no. 3 (2015): 6–9, 16–28, 38–50.

Caspari. "About Us." Last modified 2016, www.casparionline.com/About-Us. html.

Castello, Paige, and Steven Castello. Interview and tour with author, February 18, 2017.

Charlottesville Haunts and History. "Gordonsville Hotel and Hospital." Last modified November 2011, www.lodeplus.com/Charlottesville-haunts-and-history.

City of Charlottesville. "Architectural and Historic Survey." Last modified 1977, weblink.charlottesville.org/public/0/doc/652533/electronic.aspx.

City of Charlottesville. "The Farm." Last modified 2016a, www.charlottesville.org/departments-and-services/departments-h-z/neighborhood-development-services/historic-preservation-and-design-review/historic-resources-committee/historic-markers/the-farm.

City of Charlottesville. "Maplewood Cemetery." Last modified 2016b, www. charlottesville.org/departments-and-services/departments-h-z/neighborhood-development-services/historic-preservation-and-design-review/national-and-state-historic-registers/maplewood-cemetery.

Civil War Trust. "10 Facts about Brandy Station." Last modified 2014a, www. civilwar.org/battlefields/brandystation/brandy-station-history-articles/ten-facts-about-brandy.html.

Civil War Trust. "Brandy Station." Last modified 2014b, www.civilwar.org/battlefields/brandy-station.html?tab=facts.

Civil War Trust. "10 Facts about Sailor's Creek." Last modified 2014c, www. civilwar.org/battlefields/sailorscreek/sailors-creek-history-articles/ten-facts-about-sailors.html.

Civil War Trust. "The Wilderness." Last modified 2017a, www.civilwar.org/learn/civil-war/battles/wilderness.

Civil War Trust. "Overview: The Wilderness." Last modified 2017b, www.civilwar. org/learn/articles/wilderness.

Colchicine. "Afton's Palace: Swannanoa Mansion." Last modified July 2016, www. aftonmountain.com/news/afton%E2%80%99s-palace-swannanoa-mansion.

Colonial Ghosts. "18. Swannanoa Palace—Afton, Virginia." Last modified 2016, https://colonialghosts.com/Swannanoa-palace.

Conte, Cindy. Interview with author (Michie Tavern), June 22, 2016.

CookingLight. "Community Message Boards—Paranormal Experiences." Last modified April 2004, www.cookinglight.com/showthread.php?56679-paranormal-experiences&s=9cc06fa04a5404db094ba21da0743b8.

Cooper, Jean. *A Guide to Historic Charlottesville & Albemarle County, Virginia.* Charleston, SC: History Press, 2007.

De Alba, Susan. *Country Roads: Albemarle County, Virginia.* Albemarle, VA: Rockbridge, 1993.

DeLoach, Candace. Interview with author (Inn at Court Square), August 2016.

Derby, Elizabeth. "Spirited Away: An Amateur's Foray into Ghost Hunting Yields Spooky Results." Last modified October 2013, www.c-ville.com/spirited-away-an-amateurs-foray-into-ghost-hunting-yields-spooky-results.

DiMaggio, Joanne. "The Exchange Hotel: A Haunting in Gordonsville." C-ville, October 2011, www.c-ville.com/strongThe_Exchange_Hotel_A_Haunting_in_Gordonsvillestrong/#.VOPGGfkVilE.

Dove, Vee. *Madison County Homes: A Collection of Pre–Civil War Homes & Family Heritages.* Kingsport, TN: Kingsport Press, 1975.

Dulaney, James. "Swannanoa Palace." Charlottesville, VA: Skyline Swannanoa, n.d.

Earnst, Emma. "The Case of the "Not-So-Common" Comyn Hall." https://charlottesvillealbemarlehistory.wordpress.com/tag/comyn-hall.

Eastern National. "Ellwood: A Quiet Country Farm." Fort Washington, PA: Eastern National, n.d.

Elton, P. M. *Ghostly Tales of Selected Virginia State Parks.* Cambridge, MN: Adventure Publications, 2015.

Exchange Hotel. "About the Museum." Last modified 2015, www.hgiexchange.com.

Fair, Susan. "Wilderness Battlefield Apparition." Last modified October 2008, www.ghostvillage.com/encounters/2008/12012008.html.

Faust, Leo. "Can Science Find Pay-Dirt Here? Can 'Miracles' of Modern Methods Vanquish Insurmountable Obstacles of Old-Timers and Make the Gold Mines of the State Produce Again?—Experts Are Gambling That the Answer Is Yes!" *Richmond Times Dispatch*, February 9, 1936, www.facebook.com/goldrushtodd/posts/517887951555685.

Ferlazzo, Andrew. Interview and tour with author (Grass Rootes), November 2016.

Find A Grave. "William E. Isbell." www.findagrave.com/cgi-bin/fg.cgi?page=gr&GSvcid=86498&Grid=9705481&.

Fine Creek Baptist Church. "Our History." Last modified 2014, www.finecreekbaptist.org/our-history.

Foam Cage. "Haunted Pottery House." Last modified 2010, www.foamcage.com/haunted-pottery-house.

Forgotten USA. "Powhatan—Powhatan Correctional Center." Last modified 2013, http://forgottenusa.com/haunts/va/12388/powhatan_correctional_center.

Fork Union Military Academy. "Our History." www.forkunion.com/page.cfm?p=683.

Fox, Larry. "Innkeeping with the Past." *Washington Post*, March 11, 1994, www.washingtonpost.com/archive/lifestyle/1994/03/11/innkeeping-with-the-past/60752ad2-0c0d-4afc-b74b-2ed8757083C9.

Ghosts of America. "Charlottesville, Virginia Ghost Sightings—Page 3." Ghosts of America, n.d.a, www.ghostsofamerica.com/2/Virginia_Charlottesville_ghost_sightings3.html.

Ghosts of America. "Charlottesville, Virginia Ghost Sightings—Page 4." Ghosts of America, n.d.b, www.ghostsofamerica.com/2/Virginia_Charlottesville_ghost_sightings4.html.

Ghosts of America. "Charlottesville, Virginia Ghost Sightings—Page 10." Ghosts of America, n.d.c, www.ghostsofamerica.com/2/Virginia_Charlottesville_ghost_sightings10.html.

Ghosts of America. "Crozier, Virginia Ghost Sightings—Page 1." Ghosts of America, n.d.d, www.ghostsofamerica.com/2/Virginia_Crozier_ghost_sightings.html.

Ghosts of America. "Gum Springs, Virginia Ghost Sightings—Page 1." Ghosts of America, n.d.e, www.ghostsofamerica.com/2/Virginia_Gum_Soring_ghost_sightings.html.

Ghosts of America. "Louisa, Virginia Ghost Sightings—Page 4." Ghosts of America, n.d.f, www.ghostsofamerica.com/2/Virginia_Louisa_ghost_sightings4.html.

Ghosts of America. "Powhatan, Virginia Ghost Sightings—Page 4." Ghosts of America, n.d.g, www.ghostsofamerica.com/2/Virginia_powhatan_ghost_sightings4.html.

Ghosts of America. "Virginia Ghost Sightings—Bremo Bluff, Page 2." Ghosts of America, n.d.h, www.ghostsofamerica.com/2/Virginia_Bremo_Bluff_Ghost_Sightings2.html.

Ghosts of America. "Virginia Ghost Sightings—Fork Union Military Academy, Pages 1–9." Ghosts of America, n.d.i, www.ghostsofamerica.com/2/Virginia_Fork_Union_Ghost_Sightings9.html.

Ghosts of America. "Virginia Ghost Sightings—Orange, Page 2." Ghosts of America, n.d.j, www.ghostsofamerica.com/2/Virginia-orange-ghost-sightings2.html.

Godburn, Jim. Interview and tour with author (Saylor's Creek Battlefield & Hillsman House), October 2016.

Granger, Lenny. "Fire Damages Home on Stribling Avenue." *Daily Progress*, 1978, weblink.charlottesville.org/public/0/doc/652533/electronic.aspx.

Grayhaven Winery. "About Grayhaven." Last modified 2009, www.grayhavenwinery.com/html/about.html.

Gribben, Mark. "The Mayor Pays His Debt." *Malefactor's Register*, n.d., http://malefactorsregister.com/wp/the-mayor-pays-his-debt.

Hauck, Dennis. *Haunted Places: The National Directory; Ghostly Abodes, Sacred Files, UFO Landings, and Other Supernatural Locations*. New York: Penguin Books, 2002.

HauntedHouses. "Wickham Farmhouse." Last modified 2016, www.hauntedhouses.com/states/va/wickham_farmhouse.htm.

Haunted Places. "Bremo Plantation." Last modified 2016a, www.hauntedplaces. org/item/bremo-plantation.

Haunted Places. "Haunted Places in Goochland, Virginia." Last modified March 2016b, www.HauntedPlaces.org/Goochland-va.

Haunted Places. "The Inn at Willow Grove." Last modified March 2016c, www. hauntedplaces.org/item/the-inn-at-willow-grove.

Haunted Places. "Monticello." Last modified March 2016d, www.hauntedplaces. org/item/Monticello.

Haunted Places. "Amelia Wildlife Management Area." Last modified March 2016e, www.hauntedplaces.org/item/amelia-wildlife-management-area.

Haunted Places. "Haw Branch Plantation." Last modified March 2016f, www. hauntedplaces.org/item/haw-branch-plantation.

Haunted Stories. "The Screaming Woman of Haw Branch." Last modified January 2013, https://hauntedstories.net/ghost-stories/Virginia/screaming-woman- haw-branch.

Hester, Wesley. "North Pole for Sale in Crozier." *Richmond Times-Dispatch*, May 15, 2007, www.richmond.com/news/local/central-virginia/goochland/ Goochland-gazette/article_ff9e4b7e-b504-5516-b2c2-d1f18790d4C.html.

Hines, Emilee. *Virginia Myths & Legends: The True Stories Behind History's Mysteries.* 2nd ed. Guilford, CT: Globe Pequot, 2016.

Holzer, Hans. *Southern Ghosts.* New York: Tess, 1997.

Holzer, Hans. *Travel Guide to Haunted Houses: A Practical Guide to Places Haunted by Ghosts, Poltergeists, and Spirits.* New York: Black Dog & Leventhal, 1998.

Holzer, Hans. *Great American Ghost Stories.* New York: Barnes & Noble Books, 1999.

James, Sandy. "Gordonsville Depot Slated for Much-Needed Renovation." *Daily Progress*, June 3, 2016, www.dailyprogress.com/starexponent/news/ Gordonville-depot-slated-for-much-needed-renovation/article_a6ad9db4- 2907-11e6-b7d7-13809007a79e.html.

Jaquith, Waldo. "UVA to Demolish Trax, Max." *Cville News*, 2002, http:// cvillenews.com/2002/01/30/uva-to-demolish-trax-max/.

Jones, Paul. "Halloween Mystery: 99 Years Later, the McCue Murder." *The Hook*, October 2003, www.readthehook.com/92406/ cover-halloween-mystery-99- years-later-mccue-murder.

Jones, Paul. *The Hanging of Mayor McCue.* Charlottesville, VA: Priority Press, 2005.

Jones, Paul. Interview and tour with author (Old Albemarle Jail), June 4, 2016.

Journey through Hallowed Ground. "Blue Ridge Pottery." Last modified 2017, www.hallowedground.org/explore-the-journey/historic-towns-villages/ stanardsville-VA/Blue-Ridge-Pottery.

Kates, Tasha. "Ghost Tour Offers Historical Look at Maplewood." *Daily Progress*, 2011, www.dailyprogress.com/news/ghost-tour-offers-historical-look-at- maplewood/article_3310edc4-cd5d-5651-8de8-89a077458fb0.html.

Kelly, Brendan. "Viral Scary Story Claims Virginia Plantation Is Haunted by Six Murdered Boy Scouts." *Opposing Views*, January 28, 2016, www.opposingviews. com/i/social/its-easy-see-why-what-happened-six-boy-scouts-virginia-home-has-people-terrified.

Kelly, Matt. "At the University of Virginia, the Spirit of Poe Resides Evermore." *UVA Today*, July 14, 2011, https://news.virginia.edu/content/university-virginia-spirit-poe-resides-evermore.

Kinney, Pamela K. *Haunted Virginia: Legends, Myths, and True Tales*. Atglen, PA: Schiffer, 2009.

Kinney, Pamela K. *Haunted Richmond II*. Atglen, PA: Schiffer, 2012.

Koerting, Katrina. "Hauntings abound at the Mark Addy Bed & Breakfast in Nellysford." *Daily Progress*, 2012, www.dailyprogress.com/newsvirginia/ lifestyles/haunting-abound-at-mark-addy-bed-breakfast-in-nellysford/ article_66e8b983-425e-5354-9632-18a9fdfcec09.html.

Konan, Liz. Interview and tour with author, April 2016.

Kutch, Amanda. Interview and tour with author (Maplewood, Oakwood, and Riverview Cemeteries), June–August 2016.

LaLand, Patricia. *Orange County Chronicles: Stories from a Historic Virginia County*. Charleston, SC: History Press, 2011.

LandmarkHunter. "Bremo Plantation." Last modified 2016, http:// landmarkhunter.com/146379-bremo-plantation.

Library of Virginia. "Dictionary of Virginia Biography: Richard Thomas Walker Duke." www.lva.virginia.gov/public/dvb/bio.asp?b=Duke_Richard_Thomas_ Walker_1853-1926.

Long, Stephen Meriwether. "British Lieutenant Colonel Banastre Tarleton and the American Revolution: Drama on the Plantations of Charlottesville." *Meriwether Connections*, 24, nos. 1–2 (2005), http://homepages.rootsweb. ancestry.com/~meriweth/article_archive/lt_col_banastre_tarleton.html.

Louisa County. "The Green Springs National Historic Landmark District." Last modified 2015, www.louisacounty.com/LCliving/greenspr.htm.

Maddox, John. Interview with author, April 1, 2017.

Madison County Historical Society. "The Hunton House Hotel." *Preserving Yesterday Enriches Tomorrow*, November 2010, 2, www. madisonvahistoricalsociety.org/newsletter%20November%202010.pdf.

Madison County Historical Society. "The Kemper Residence." Madison, VA: Eddins Ford, n.d.

Mark Addy Inn. "History of the Mark Addy." Last modified 2016, www.mark-addy.com/history.

Maurer, David. "Set in Stone: The Serenity of UVA's Cemetery Belies a Colorful Past." *UVA Magazine*, Spring 2008, http://uvamagazine.org/articles/set_in_ stone.

Mayhurst Inn. "Mayhurst Inn: Much More Than a Perfect Getaway." Last modified 2017a, www.mayhurstinn.com.

Mayhurst Inn. "Points of History." Last modified 2017b, www.mayhurstinn.com/about#points-of-history.

McFarland, Laura. "Local Prison to Close in Wake of Cuts." *Powhatan Today*, October 15, 2014, www.richmond.com/news/local/central-virginia/powhatan/powhatan-today/article-b837ac14-54d8-11e4-ab61-001a4bcf6878.htm.

McFarland, Laura. "Shiloh Baptist Church Celebrates 150th Anniversary." *Powhatan Today*, October 6, 2016, www.richmond.com/news/local/central-virginia/powhatan/powhatan-today/shiloh-baptist-church-celebrates-th-anniversary/article_7alecd40-8b3b-11e6-9933-b30517a41411.html.

McKendry, David Ian. "Six Boy Scouts Murdered by a Witch Still Haunt a Virginia Road." *Blumhouse*, January 25, 2016a, www.blumhouse.com/2016/01/25/six-boy-scouts-murdered-by-a-witch-still-haunt-a-virginia-road.

McKendry, David Ian. "You Can Still Hear the Screams of People Being Buried Alive: The Ghosts of Virginia's Wilderness Battlefield." Last modified March 29, 2016b, www.blumhouse.com/2016/03/29/you-can-still-hear-the-screams-of-people-burning-alive-the-ghosts-of-virginias-wilderness-battlefield.

McKenna, Marla. "A Spirited Group: Culpeper Paranormal Investigates Local Haunts." *Daily Progress*, October 2016, www.dailyprogress.com/starexponent/news/a-spirited-group-culpeper-paranormal-investigates-local-haunts/article_720ac076-ba80-528c-b568*723d5ff13860.html.

Miller, Charles, and Peter Miller. *Monticello: The Official Guide to Thomas Jefferson's World*. Washington, DC: National Geographic Society, 2016.

Mills, Teresa. "Ghosts and Haunted Houses in Madison Virginia." Last modified 2000, www.teresamills.bizland.com/ghosts/text/text.html.

Mindat.org. "Gold-Pyrite Belt, Goochland Co., Virginia, USA." Last modified January 2015, www.mindat.org/loc-105393.html.

Miss May. Interview and tour with author (Michie Tavern), June 22, 2016.

Moseley, Lucille. "The Huguenot Society of the Founders of Manakin in the Colony of Virginia." Last modified February 2016, http://huguenot-manakin.org/houses/houses.php?house=20.

Mucci, Dan. "Old Woodville in Historic Green Mountain District." Last modified April 2015, www.mcleanfalconer.com/mcleanfalconer-com-blog/2015/04/06/old-woodville-in-historic-green-mountain-district.

Nunley, Debbie, and Karen Jane Elliott. *A Taste of Virginia History: A Guide to Historic Eateries and Their Recipes*. Winston-Salem, NC: John F. Blair, 2004.

Oakland School. "The Grounds." Last modified 2017a, http://oaklandschool.net/grounds.

Oakland School. "Oakland History." Last modified 2017b, http://oaklandschool.net/Oakland-history.

O'Bryant, Margaret. Interview (Albemarle Historical Society), July 20, 2016.

Our Roots. "About Us." Last modified 2017, www.lafayette.com/aboutus.

Oyster Ranch. "Oyster Ranching Etc.: Murders, Whores, Wars and Healing Waters; A Non Jeffersonian Tour of Charlottesville." Last modified May 9,

2011, http://oysterranch.blogspot.com/2011/05/murders-whores-wars-and-healing-waters.html.

Penne Lane Caterers. "About Penne Lane." Last modified 2011, http://pennelane-troymarket.com/About_Penne_Lane.html.

Powell, Lewis O., IV. "Begowned Ghosts—Higher Ed Haunts of Virginia." In *Southern Spirit Guide: A Guide to the Ghosts and Hauntings of the American South* (blog). Last modified September 15, 2014, http://southernspiritguide.blogspot.com/2014/09/begowned-ghostshigher-ed-haunts-of.html.

Presidential Avenue. "Zachary Taylor, 12th President, 1849–1850." Last modified 2012, www.presidentialavenue.com/zt.cfm.

Preston, Daniel. *A Narrative of the Life of James Monroe with a Chronology.* Charlottesville, VA: Ash Lawn–Highland, 2011.

Providence Presbyterian Church. "Our History." https://providencepc.wordpress.com/our-history.

Puccio, Lindsay. "Real Haunted School in Charlottesville?" Last modified October 2005, www.newsplex.com/home/headlines/1935407.html.

Rainville, Lynn. "Maplewood Cemetery." Last modified 2011, www2.vcdh.virginia.edu/cem/db/cemetery/details/mpw.

Rathbone Emma. "There's Something Strange in Your Neighborhood." *UVA Magazine*, October 13, 2013, http://uvamagazine.org/articles/theres_something_strange_in_your_neighborhood.

Richmond, James. "Anyone for Ghosts?" Goochland Historical Society. Last modified October 2015, https://goochlandhistory.wordpress.com/tag/james-river-correctional-center.

Sailor's Creek Battlefield Historical State Park. *Lee's Retreat—the Final Campaigns: Driving Tour Loop of the Battles of Sailor's Creek.* Rice, VA: Virginia Department of Conservation & Recreation, n.d.

Sancken, Kristin. "Ghostly Legends of Fluvanna County." *Fluvanna Review*, October 27, 2010, www.fluvannareview.com/index.php?id=1146:ghostly-legends-of-fluvanna-county&option=com_content.

Sausmikat, Rita. Interview and tour with author (Tuckahoe Plantation), April 26, 2016.

Scherquist, Lena. Interview and tour with author (Salubria Manor), November 11, 2016.

Scott, Kevin. Interview and tour with author (Grass Rootes), November 2016.

Shadowlands Haunted Places Index. "Haunted Places in Virginia." Last modified 1998, www.theshadowlands.net/places/virginia.htm.

Sherman, Anita. "Grass Rootes: Showcasing Farm-to-Table Cuisine." *Culpeper Times*, March 5, 2017, www.culpepertimes.com/2017/03/05/grass-rootes-showcasing-farm-to-table-cuisine/159762.

Shiloh Baptist Church. "The History of Shiloh Baptist Church." Last modified 2016, www.welcometoshiloh.com/history-of-the-church.

Sinclair, Melissa Scott. "Sacred Ground: Three Nuns Seek Allies to Help Bring New Life to a Forgotten Paradise in Powhatan." *Style Weekly*, May 10, 2006, www.styleweekly.com/Richmond/sacred-ground/content?oid=1368481.

Sincock, J. Morgan. *America's Early Taverns: Food, Drink, Lodging and Hospitality along the Nation's Early Roadways.* Lebanon, PA: Applied Arts, 1992.

Smith, Denise. Interview with author (Graffiti House), October 30, 2016.

Steger, Martha. "A Ghost Story at Tuckahoe Plantation." *Goochland Gazette*, October 20, 2010, http://media.mgnetwork.com/glg/archive/102110RSGA.pdf.

Strange USA. "Tandem Friends School." Last modified September 2008, www.strangeusa.com/ViewLocation.aspx?id=10271&desc=_tandem_friends_school__Charlottesville__VA&x=1.

Swannanoa Palace: Haunted and Mournful. Last modified December 2012, www.poptug.com/Swannanoa-palace-haunted-and-mournful.

Sykes, Missy. Interview and tour with author (Civil War Exchange Hotel), March 4, 2017.

Tal, Jen. Interview and tour with author (Mark Addy Inn), October 9, 2016.

Tandem Friends. "History." Last modified 2016, www.tandemfs.org/page/about/history.

Taylor, John. "A Guide to Virginia's Presidential Estates and Plantations." *Washington Post*, May 14, 2015, www.washingtonpost.com/goingoutguide/Virginias-presidential-estates-a-planning-guide/2015/05/14/9d9bbf80-f7ee-11e4-9ef4-1bb7ce3b3fb7_story.html?utm_term=.7dd74b99ddf8.

Taylor, L. B., Jr. *The Ghosts of Fredericksburg and Nearby Environs.* Lynchburg, VA: Progress Printing, 1991.

Taylor, L. B., Jr. *The Ghosts of Charlottesville and Lynchburg and Nearby Environs.* Lynchburg, VA: Progress Printing, 1992.

Taylor, L. B., Jr. *Civil War Ghosts of Virginia.* Lynchburg, VA: Progress Printing, 2007.

Taylor, L. B., Jr. *Haunted Virginia: Ghosts and Strange Phenomena of the Old Dominion.* Mechanicsburg, PA: Stackpole Books, 2009.

Taylor, L. B., Jr. *The Big Book of Virginia Ghost Stories.* Mechanicsburg, PA: Stackpole Books, 2010.

Thomas Jefferson Monticello. "Timeline of the Founding of the University of Virginia." Last modified July 2011, www.monticello.org/site/research-and-collections/timeline-founding-university-virginia.

Thompson, Addison. *Tuckahoe Plantation.* Goochland, VA: Tuckahoe Plantation Enterprises, 1997.

Tidewater Paranormal. "Virginia Battlefields." Last modified 2013, www.tidewaterparanormal.yolasite.com/battlefields.php.

Tomlin, Jackie. "Haunting at Sailor's Creek." Last modified August 2010, www.ms-swami.com/sailorscreek.html.

Trevilian Station. "June 11–12, 1864 Battle." Trevilian Station, n.d.a, www.trevilianstation.org/battle.htm.

Trevilian Station. "Driving Tour." Trevilian Station, n.d.b, www.trevilian station. org/tour.htm.

Tribble, Todd, and Kendra Tribble. Interview and tour with author (Tribble Farm & Home), July 3, 2016.

True Ghost Tales. "Virginia Prison Spirit." Last modified 2013, www. trueghosttales.com/paranormal/virginia-prison-spirit.

Tuckahoe Plantation c. 1733: The Boyhood Home of Thomas Jefferson. Goochland, VA: Tuckahoe Plantation Enterprises, n.d.

Twisted Paranormal Society. "Mount Eagle Farm." Last modified 2015a, https:// twistedparanormal society.com/Mount_Eagle_Farm.php.

Twisted Paranormal Society. "Swannanoa Mansion." Last modified 2015b, https://twistedparanormalsociety.com/Swannanoa-mansion.php.

United States Department of the Interior. "National Register of Historic Places Inventory: Sunny Bank." Last modified April 1976, www.dhr.virginia.gov/ registers/counties/Albemarle/002-0096-SunnyBank-1976-finalnomination.pdf.

University of Virginia. "Lawn." Last modified 2016, www.virginia.edu/housing/ options.php?id=lawn&type=upperclass.

Viccellio, Robert. "Ghoulish Grounds: Hair-Raising Tales from Around the University." *UVA Magazine*, October 16, 2012, http://uvamagazine.org/articles/ ghoulish_grounds.

Virginia Beach Family Fun. "Tour Swannanoa—the Lost Haunted House on a Hill." Last modified 2015, www.virginia-beach-family-fun.com/Swannanoa.html.

Virginia Department of Corrections. "Department of Corrections Brief History." Last modified 2016a, https://vadoc.virginia.gov/about/history.shtm.

Virginia Department of Corrections. "PREA Audit Report." Last modified August 2016b, https://vadoc.virginia.gov/about/facts/default.shtm.

Virginia Department of Education. "Gordon-Barbour Elementary." http:// schoolquality.virginia.gov/schools/gordon-barbour-elementary.

Virginia Department of Game and Inland Fisheries. "Amelia WMA." Last modified 2016, www.dgif.virginia.gov/wma/Amelia.

Virginia Estates. "Edgewood Farm and Estate." Last modified 2016, www. virginiaestates.com/edgewood.

Virginia Haunted Houses. "Haw Branch Plantation—Real Haunted Place." Last modified 2016, www.virginiahauntedhouses.com/real-haunt/haw-branch-plantation.html.

Virginia Historic Landmark. "Jerdone Castle." www.revolvy.com/topic/ Jerdone%20Castle&uid=1575.

Virginia Tourism Corporation. "Historic Sites: Belmead Mansion." Last modified 2016, www.virginia.org/listings/historicsites/belmeadmansion.

Virginia's Rockhounder. "Rockhounding in Goochland County, Virginia." https:// varockshop.com/rockhounding/rockhound-info/field-collecting/collecting-on-your-own-in-virginia/rockhounding-in-goochland-county-virginia/.

Woodard Properties. "Open House at Comyn Hall." Last modified 2011, woodardproperties.com/news/open-house-at-comyn-hall.

INDEX

Susan Schwartz has been an avid writer for ten years, writing about the paranormal, writing freelance articles, editing manuscripts, and proofing medical competencies. In addition to publishing three stories in the anthologies of Nightmare & Echoes I, II, and III, Susan is a member of the Horror Writers Association and the Virginia Writers Club, where she serves as President of the Richmond Chapter. She also has two novels in the works: a paranormal romance and a medical thriller. In her spare time, she loves to read, travel to foreign lands, and traipse through old graveyards. Please leave feedback at www.susanschwartzauthor.com or Ncc17lu@aol.com.

Cliff Middlebrook Jr. began taking pictures of trains and various railroad settings. As his photography skills grew, he branched out into landscapes, sunrises and sunsets, and architecture. His photographs have been published in several magazines and books in Great Britain and the United States; they are also displayed in businesses and homes across the country. Visit Cliff's website at: https://fineartamerica.com/artists/cliff+middlebrook.

Author Susan Schwartz and her brother, photographer Cliff Middlebrook Jr.

MY SIGHTINGS

LOCATION:

_____

_____

_____

_____

DATE/TIME/CONDITIONS:

_____

_____

_____

_____

EXPERIENCE:

_____

_____

_____

_____

_____

_____

_____

_____

Location:

_____
_____
_____

Date/Time/Conditions:

_____
_____
_____

Experience:

_____
_____
_____
_____
_____
_____
_____
_____
_____

LOCATION:

_____

_____

_____

DATE/TIME/CONDITIONS:

_____

_____

_____

EXPERIENCE:

_____

_____

_____

_____

_____

_____

_____

_____